Uncle John's

by the Bathroom Readers' Institute

Bathroom Readers' Press
Ashland, Oregon

UNCLE JOHN'S SMELL-O-SCOPIC BATHROOM READER® FOR KIDS ONLY

For information, write:
The Bathroom Readers' Institute
P.O. Box 1117
Ashland, OR 97520
www.bathroomreader.com

Cover design and illustration by Pete Whitehead
Interior illustration by Nicholas R. Halliday

ISBN-10: 1-60710-780-5 / ISBN-13: 978-1-60710-780-4

Library of Congress Cataloging-in-Publication Data
Uncle John's smell-o-scopic bathroom reader for kids only!
    pages cm
    ISBN 978-1-60710-780-4 (pbk.)
    1. Wit and humor, juvenile. 2. Curiosities and wonders--
Juvenile literature. I. Bathroom Readers' Institute (Ashland,
Or.) II. Title: Smell-o-scopic bathroom reader for kids only!
    PN6166.U55 2013
    081.02'07--dc23
                                        2012043855

Printed in the United States of America
First Printing: 2013

17 16 15 14 13   6 5 4 3 2 1

THANK YOU!

The Bathroom Readers' Institute sincerely thanks those whose creative efforts made this book possible.

Gordon Javna

Kim T. Griswell

Jay Newman

Brian Boone

Trina Janssen

Pete Whitehead

Nick Halliday

Carly Schuna

Rich Wallace

Kelly Milner Halls

Mark Haverstock

Nancy Coffelt

Molly Marcot

Elizabeth Armstrong Hall

Joan M. Kyzer

Megan Todd

J. Carroll

Molly Glover

Melinda Allman

JoAnn Padgett

Aaron Guzman

Mana Manzavi

Ginger Winters

Jennifer Frederick

R. R. Donnelley

Publishers Group West

Amanda Halliday

Manny, Cocoa, and Felix

The Evo's Gang

Thomas Crapper

*　　*　　*

There isn't enough space to list the names of the thousands of kids who have written to the BRI, but without you, this book would have been impossible.

TABLE OF CONTENTS

Because the BRI understands your reading needs, we've
divided the contents by length as well as subject:
Short—A quick read
Medium—2 pages
Long—3 to 5 pages (that's not too long, is it?)

IT'S A MOUTHFUL

JUST FOR FUN

MYTHS & LEGENDS

MOUTHING OFF

LIFE IS STRANGE

STORM WARNING

*   *   *

GREETINGS FROM UNCLE JOHN

FFLLBBLLLTTT!

Hey! Which one of you kids did that? Was it you? Wait...nevermind. It was the dog.

So, let's cut to the chase (as opposed to cutting the cheese)—this book smells! It's filled with pulsating sewer worms, farting beetles, and astronauts who don't change their underwear for a week. (We're not kidding!) Dare to open this book and you'll read about stinking gourds and sweaty feet, smelly aliens and armpit musicians. Nothing (and I mean nothing) is too smelly for *Uncle John's Smell-O-Scopic Bathroom Reader*, and it's FOR KIDS ONLY!

Of course, this book isn't only about what the nose knows! The brain wants in on the action. (The intestines do too, but they'll have to wait their turn.) For the past year, BRI writers around the country and in the little red house in Ashland, Oregon, have been working overtime. We've used our schnozes to sniff out true stories and fascinating facts that will tantalize your senses and AMAZE YOUR BRAIN.

What weirdness and wonders await inside *Uncle John's Smell-O-Scopic Bathroom Reader FOR KIDS ONLY?*

- A billionaire who blows fire from his mouth
- Where to go if you want to throw Brussels sprouts at people (and not get arrested)
- Know-it-all experts who were very very wrong
- An airline safety agent who quarantined a cupcake but gave a chainsaw the OK to fly
- Toy ideas so terrible you won't believe they're real
- A plug at the bottom of the Baltic Sea
- The latest study on texting in the toilet
- What else? Mammoth jokes, video-gamer speak, cartoon characters, dumb sports stars, ocean floaters, Bigfoot's cousins, comic geniuses, kid geniuses, musical geniuses, and Dr. Fart, the perfect medical genius for a Smell-O-Scopic bathroom reader!

I hope you find something brain buzzing (and nose-tingling) in this book. And I hope you share your newfound knowledge with your friends. That's what we do every day at the Bathroom Readers' Institute, and we've been doing it for 26 years! From all of us here—including Manny, our favorite farting dog—here's to smell-o-riffic reading, and remember:

No matter where you go…

…Go with the Flow!

——Uncle John and the BRI staff

SMELL-O-TRIVIA

The nose knows…and so will you, after you read these fascinating facts about the sense of smell.

• Astronauts lose their sense of smell in space.

• A dog has about 300 million smell receptors in its nose, while a human has just 5 million.

• There's a name for losing your sense of smell: *anosmia.* If you're born with no sense of smell, you have *congenital anosmia.* About 1 in 50,000 girls and 1 in 10,000 boys have it.

• Scientists think that couples who have been together for years can smell each other's emotions…in their sweat.

• Sniffing something that smells good actually has the power to lift your mood. (Next time you're grumpy, tell your mom all she has to do to change your mood is bake a batch of chocolate-chip cookies.)

• Believe it or not, babies can smell, to a limited degree, when they're in the womb. They pick up odors from their mothers' food and drink, and studies have shown that they like sweet things best.

• What you smell can affect your dreams. One study found that people who smelled rotten eggs had more nightmares.

Stinkiest mushroom species: the stinkhorn.

TATTOOED PITS

...and other wacky habits from human history.

Aaahh.... That feels better!!

- Mayans and other ancient peoples practiced a medical procedure called *trepanation*—drilling a hole into a person's skull to "relieve" headaches and seizures.

- In Ancient Greece, sneezing was seen as a good omen, sent by the gods.

- Soldiers in Hitler's army had their blood types tattooed in their armpits. Why? In case they got hurt during battle and needed a transfusion.

- That leafy wreath Julius Caesar is always pictured wearing? He wore it to cover up his balding head.

- Ancient Egyptians shaved their eyebrows when their cats passed away.

- One Russian emperor had men with beards pay a tax for their beards. Those who paid the tax had to carry a "beard token" with them to prove it.

- Married women in Japan used to dye their teeth black to show their loyalty to their husbands.

A dollar bill can be folded in the same spot 4,000 times before it tears.

SILLY CELEBS

This just in: Famous people are weird.

"I'm thinking of buying a monkey. Then I think, 'Why stop at one?' I don't like being limited in that way."

—**Robert Downey, Jr.**

"I'm obsessed with shoes. I must have hundreds of pairs. I'm a shoe fiend. That reminds me—I need to go shopping!"

—**Keira Knightley**

"I want to be a doctor, a nurse, a hair saloner, a makeup saloner, work at Wal-Mart, work at Kmart, work at McDonald's where I can eat all the chicken nuggets, and work at a hotel so I can go swimming."

—**Honey Boo-Boo**

"I pretty much try to stay in a constant state of confusion just because of the expression it leaves on my face."

—**Johnny Depp**

"I unfortunately still crave Chicken McNuggets and bacon, which is the meat candy of the world."

—**Katy Perry**

"It's kind of hard to balance school and work sometimes. But sometimes, like, if I'm going to the White House and I'm in there doing a tour and stuff, that's like school."

—**Justin Bieber**

R.I.P
LONESOME
GEORGE

Think bringing back an extinct species only happens in movies like Jurassic Park*? This story could change your mind.*

WHY SO LONESOME?

In June of 2012, Lonesome George, a world-famous Pinta Island tortoise, died. Lonesome George had a long life on the Galápagos Islands off the coast of Ecuador. No one knows exactly how long George lived. The giant tortoise was full-grown when he was found and captured in 1972. But he's believed to have lived at least 100 years.

Despite his long life, conservationists had been dreading his death. Why? There was a reason Lonesome George was lonesome: He was the last known member of his subspecies. For the last 40 years of his life, George lived alone. And his death meant the extinction of the Pinta Island tortoise. Or did it?

HUNGER GAMES

Just months after Lonesome George died, Yale University researchers announced a discovery. On nearby Isabela Island, they had found 17 tortoises that carried some of the same DNA as the Pinta Island subspecies. Lonesome George's subspecies might not be extinct after all.

Isabela and Pinta islands are separated by about 37 miles of open ocean. So how, researchers wondered, did the Pinta Island tortoises get there? They probably could not have swum or floated that far. The most likely explanation is that they were carried to Isabela by fishermen or pirates.

SWIM FOR YOUR LIVES!

In the 1800s, sailors hungry for protein hunted the giant tortoises that lived on the Galápagos Islands. They often took the animals aboard their ships as they sailed from island to island. In fact, they took so many that they started the tortoises on the road to extinction.

Researchers believe that a few Pinta Island tortoises may have been thrown overboard near Isabela Island and some swam to safety. If so, that means the hungry fishermen and pirates who caused the decline of Lonesome George's subspecies may have also saved it.

The road back won't be easy. Officials at the Galápagos National Park say the hybrids on Isabela could be bred to resurrect Lonesome George's subspecies. But bringing back the Pinta Island tortoise through selective breeding will take between 100 and 150 years.

BATHROOM LORE

*A few little-known facts about the room
you might be sitting in right now.*

THE WHOLE HOG

A classic "claw-foot" tub is deep and luxurious. It's made of porcelain-coated cast iron and sits atop four metal legs that curve into clawed feet. Claw-foot tubs were bathroom queens in the Victorian age (late 1800s to early 1900s). But their beginnings were surprisingly humble. In the 1800s, a lot of farmers used "hog tubs" to briefly boil pigs that had been slaughtered for meat. A quick boil made it easier to scrape off the pig's hair. (Let's face it; no one wants bristles in the bacon.)

In 1883, John Kohler decided he could build a better hog tub. He coated an iron tub with enamel, gave it a name (the Hog Scalder), and traded it to a farmer for one cow and 14 chickens. Kohler advertised his enameled tubs for use as horse troughs, hog scalders, and—with the addition of four legs with clawed feet—bathtubs.

CREATURE FROM THE SEWERS

In 2009, a contractor working in Raleigh, North Carolina, took video footage of a "sewer monster" living in the sanitation system and posted the clip on YouTube. The pink-brown, blobbish creature appeared to pulsate like a beating heart or a quivering lung. Within a week, the video had more than 5 million views—but no one could figure out what it was.

Then biologists at the Raleigh Public Utilities Department analyzed the video. They concluded that the creature wasn't a single monster. It was a monstrous colony of tubifex worms. And the "heartbeat"? That, they decided, was the worms convulsing in response to the camera's light. *Tubifex tubifex* is a kind of segmented worm that lives in the sludge of lakes, rivers, and—so it seems—sewer systems. It can digest bacteria and thrive in polluted areas that would kill other species.

Mystery solved. Or was it? Another biologist made a different assessment. He thought the monster was a colony of *bryozoans*, tiny invertebrates that form bloblike masses with tentacles. In the end, no one knew for sure what beast was living in the sewers of Raleigh, North Carolina. But health officials decided the "sewer monster" could stay put. Since it wasn't blocking the pipes, it didn't pose any harm.

There's a fruit called "stinking toe."

TERRIBLE TOYS

*Further proof that some adults have…uhm…
questionable ideas about what kids like.*

BABY WEE WEE

Baby Wee Wee was the brainchild of a Spanish toy company called Famosa. Starting in 2007, the doll was sold for a limited time in the United Kingdom for £40 (about $65). The doll came with a plastic bottle and a plastic potty. After revving Baby Wee Wee up with a couple of batteries, you would fill his bottle with water and help him "drink." You can imagine what happens next: he has to pee. But you might not be able to imagine what the doll does: he starts grabbing his crotch. That's when you haul out the potty, pull down his pants, and watch him go. In 2008, Famosa released an even more disturbing doll, Baby Pirulin Pee Pee. This one has a "little willy" that moves when he pees.

MY CLEANING TROLLEY

This toy was supposed to make cleaning feel like child's play. The trolley looks like a tiny, more colorful version of one you might see a hotel housecleaner truck around. It features a broom, mop, brush, dustpan, bucket, and working vacuum cleaner. The set has been redesigned since its original release in 2009, but that first version angered feminists around the world because it had all pink equipment and stated "GIRLS ONLY" on the box.

By your 10th birthday, you'll have worn out, on average, 730 crayons.

PLAYMOBIL© SECURITY CHECK POINT

Most travelers don't think going through airport security is fun. Playmobil© apparently thinks it's child's play. In 2003, the company released the Security Check Point play set. Inside: a traveler figure, two Transportation Security Administration figures, a scanner doorway, and an X-ray machine belt. Just in case the traveler tries something funny, the two officers are equipped with plastic guns. As it turns out, even people who run toy stores think the Playmobil© Security Check Point is a bad idea. "The best toys are open-ended to foster imagination, while a security check point can never be," says one toy store owner.

ROADKILL TOYS

Roadkill toys, otherwise known as "squash plush," are soft stuffed animals from a British toy manufacturer that look like they've been—you guessed it—run over by a car. Tire tracks cross their backs. Their "guts" and tongues hang out. And their bloodshot eyes stare at…well, nothing, since they're dead. Each plush animal comes with a body bag, a death certificate, and an identity tag. Fuzzy (but… dead) friends include Smudge the Squirrel, Twitch the Raccoon, Grind the Rabbit, and Fender the Fox.

The brain weighs about three times as much as the heart.

STINKY BUGS

These creatures put their bodily emissions to good use.

THE FART RIDE: Next time you're in a pool, see if your farts are as powerful as those of the rove beetle. This long skinny beetle releases a chemical gas from its rear end that can actually move it across the surface of a pond. How? The tiny gas bubble rapidly expands and pushes the beetle in front of it.

THIS BEETLE'S SMOKIN': The bombardier beetle is another champion farter. It defends itself by squirting explosive gas at attackers. The gas comes out with a loud pop and a cloud of blue smoke. These bug bombs are so hot they can actually raise blisters on other creatures. And the smell? The heat makes it extra strong. But these farts are no accident. The bombardier beetle carefully controls its gas, letting it go in small, short bursts: up to 80 farts in 4 minutes.

READY, AIM, FIRE: The two-striped walking stick doesn't exactly fart. When threatened, it takes careful aim and then shoots wet smelly gunk out of glands behind its head. The smell is so disgusting its victims can hardly breathe. Some say it can even make a person faint.

An egg of the extinct elephant bird could make an omelet...

UNDERWEAR IN SPACE

*Amaze your friends with facts about life in space
that you'll never learn in school.*

ONE SIZE FITS ALL

Early space capsules were small. How small? The 1960s-era Mercury capsule was so tiny only one astronaut could fit in it at a time. "It was worn," joked the astronauts, "not ridden."

POOP BAGS

Captain Jim Lovell once described living in a space capsule as "a lot like living in a Porta-Potty." Why? The dreaded fecal bag. "You didn't have a toilet in the Gemini and Apollo capsules," said Mary Roach, author of *Packing for Mars*. "Just a bag." So when a capsule splashed down at the end of a mission and the frogmen opened the hatch, the smell was—as Lovell politely put it—"quite different than the fresh ocean breezes outside."

POPCORN POOPING

Space shuttles do have toilets, but…"It's very cold in there," said Roach. "All the material freezes and tends to bounce around off the sides, and, because it's zero

gravity, it makes its way back up out of the toilet."
Shuttle toilets include "rearview mirrors" so astronauts
can check to make sure no little bits escaped. Those bits
are called *fecal popcorn*.

THE URINE DUMP

The memoirs of at least three American astronauts
say that one of the most beautiful things to see from a
capsule is the snowy sparkle of urine ejected into space.
When "flushed" into space, drops of pee freeze instantly,
and a silvery snowstorm swirls around the capsule.

LONG JOHNS IN SPACE

Instead of wearing those uncomfortable spacesuits all
day and night, astronauts aboard *Gemini 7* took the suits
off and journeyed home in their long johns. Afterward,
Captain Jim Lovell's son spread the story that "Dad
orbited Earth in his underwear."

STATIC CLING

Astronauts aboard *Apollo 12* discovered something
irritating about moon dust: it clings! Moon dust—also
known as *lunar regolith*—has a static charge. Back on
Earth, that wouldn't be a problem. Why? Because
Earth's magnetic field wards off charged particles. But
the moon doesn't have a global magnetic field. So all
that dust clings "like socks in the drier." After taking
a few small steps on the moon, the astronauts were so
covered with moon dust they looked like miners. Then

they tracked all that dust into the space capsule. Pretty soon it was everywhere—even in their underwear. Talk about uncomfortable. What did they do? Crew members stripped naked and headed back to Earth in their birthday suits.

What color was dinosaurs' skin? Nobody knows.

IF THE NAME FITS...

An "aptronym" is a name that matches the job of its owner in a way that makes you laugh. Here are a few of our real-life favorites.

Linda Toot: flute player in the Milwaukee Symphony Orchestra

Professor Martin Braine: psychologist

Lake Speed: NASCAR driver

George Hammer: hardware store owner

Dr. David Toothaker: dentist

Bruce Sparks: electrician

Dan Druff: barber

Sara Blizzard: weather forecaster

Edmund Akenhead: crossword puzzle editor for the *London Times*

Roland Cruz: auto mechanic

Cardinal Jaime Sin: former head of Catholic church in the Philippines

Jim Kiick: football player

Colin Bass: bass player

Dr. I. Doctor: ophthalmologist

Anna Smashnova: tennis player

James Bugg: exterminator

Robert Killingbeck: chiropractor

David Dollar: economist

John Lawless: policeman

Sue Yoo: attorney

SCRAMBLED BRAINS

Here's an easy way to eat like a zombie.

WHAT YOU NEED:

INGREDIENTS

- ½ block of silken tofu
- ¼ tsp. garlic or onion powder
- ¼ tsp. salt
- Pepper, to taste
- ½ T. olive oil
- Ketchup

SUPPLIES

- Bowl
- Frying pan
- Spatula
- Plate

WHAT TO DO:

1. Plop the tofu into a bowl. Mash it with your fingers until it looks like scrambled brains.
2. Add the garlic or onion powder, salt, and pepper. Mash in the seasonings.
3. Set the stove burner to medium heat. With an adult's help, warm a frying pan. Pour in the olive oil, and add the brain mixture. Toss it with a spatula so it doesn't stick to the pan.
4. When the brains start to firm up (about 5 minutes), empty them onto a plate and serve sprinkled with ketchup "blood."

A banana will typically travel 4,000 miles before it's eaten.

ASK THE EXPERTS

There will always be more questions than answers, but here are a couple you can stop scratching your head about.

D
ON'T FORGET TO BRUSH!
Q: *How clean is your toothbrush?*
A: "It may surprise you to know that bacteria can thrive on toothbrushes. Toothbrushes provide the bacteria with lots of food and water. The two most commonly found germs on used toothbrushes are *staphylococci* (which can cause boils and lesions) and *streptococci* (throat and other infections). Researchers have also found the viruses for influenza and herpes simplex on toothbrushes. It makes a big difference where you keep your toothbrush. There's a risk of contamination if it's too near the toilet. When we flush, water droplets containing more than 25,000 virus particles and 600,000 bacteria spray into the air. These droplets have been found as far as 20 feet from the toilet. One solution is to put the lid down before flushing." (From *Why Fish Fart* by Francesca Gould)

NO BLUE SKIN

Q: *Why isn't our skin green or blue?*
A: "The color of human skin is caused by a pigment called *melanin*. This pigment determines how dark the skin will be. People who don't have a lot of melanin have white, fair skin. People who have a lot of melanin

---

A mouse can squeeze through a hole the size of a piece of popped popcorn.

have dark, black skin. But there are no purple, green, or blue pigments in human skin. So you can't have purple, green, or blue skin...at least, not naturally." (From *Why Don't Your Eyelashes Grow?* by Beth Ann Ditkoff, M.D.)

BIRD ON A WIRE

Q: *Why don't birds get shocked when they sit on wires?*

A: "That does look surprising. Birds sometimes sit on wires carrying thousands of volts. Living things, like birds and people, can get shocked by touching two different wires or touching one wire and the ground. Then electricity has a way in and out, and can flow through a body and give a dangerous shock. A bird on an electric wire is safe and happy—unless it makes the mistake of touching another wire at the same time. Then it's a dead bird." (from *Highlights Book of Science Questions* by Jack Myers, Ph.D.)

BOO!

Q: *Why do we turn pale when we're spooked?*

A: "Just as there are nerves that dilate blood vessels, there are nerves that contract them. These latter nerves are called *vasoconstrictor* nerves. During a sudden scare or fright, the constrictor nerves become stimulated and cause the blood vessels to contract. Thus, the supply of blood is lessened, and the result is a pallor." (*How a Fly Walks Upside Down* by Martin M. Goldwyn.)

THAT'S GROSS: HAIR EDITION

Hair: It's here, there, and everywhere…except on Uncle John's head, where he thinks it should be.

HAIRWEAR

Sweaters, hats, gloves, scarves…all kinds of wearables can be made from yarn. And yarn can be spun from all kinds of hair: sheep, goat, cow, deer, buffalo, rabbit, even human hair. Carol Kroll is one of a small group of knitters who use human hair to spin yarn and make clothing and other wearables. Kroll claims yarn spun from human hair is very strong. It can be soft and smooth, or prickly and whiskery, depending on the texture of the hair and how it's spun. To make human-hair yarn, just dampen the strands of hair, twist them, smooth down any pesky "whiskers," and spin the strands together until they form a coil. According to Kroll, the most popular hairwear items right now are watchbands, bracelets, rings, and necklaces.

FOUL BALL

Ever wonder why your bathroom drain keeps clogging? Hair is probably the culprit. It's made of keratin, a protein that is insoluble (doesn't dissolve) in water.

Keratin is the same stuff that makes up your fingernails and horses' hooves. Some hairy drain clumps can swell to the size of baseballs!

BWAWK IT UP, BUDDY

Hairy clumps that end up in the digestive system instead of a drain have a different name—*trichobezoars*—a fancy word for hairballs. Cats are infamous for coughing them up, but oxen, llamas, horses, rabbits, and even chickens can have them. Wait—chickens don't have hair! True, but that doesn't stop them from eating it. The National Museum of Health and Medicine in Silver Springs, Maryland, has a chicken hairball on display to prove it. The bird in question was a pet that became buddies with the family dog. Then it started plucking out the dog's fur and swallowing it. The hair mass in the chicken's gut grew so large it couldn't eat. The mass had to be surgically removed. Good news: The chicken lived to peck another day.

RATS OKAY WITH FDA

When you take a bite out of your next PB&J, keep this in mind: The odds are good there's a rat hair in there. According to the Food and Drug Administration (FDA), an average 400-gram jar of peanut butter has about four rodent hairs in it. Your run-of-the-mill box of macaroni probably contains more than seven rodent hairs, and more than 50 percent of popcorn samples are hiding at least one rodent hair. Good news, though—all of those levels are deemed acceptable by the FDA.

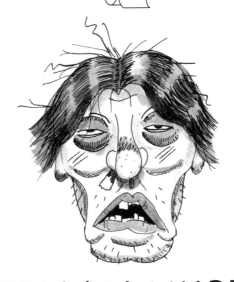

WORLD'S DUMBEST SPORTS INJURIES

Not every sports injury can be linked to striving for athletic excellence. Some are just plain dumb.

ANGER MISMANAGEMENT

In April 2012, New York Knicks All-Star forward Amar'e Stoudemire missed a key playoff game against the Miami Heat. He couldn't play because he had 15 stitches in his right hand. He didn't slice it open on the backboard or stumble over a photographer on the court. The Knicks lost a playoff game to the Heat by ten points, and Stoudemire took out his anger on the glass door covering a fire extinguisher outside the locker room. The player left the arena with his arm in a sling, but still able to type. "Not proud of my actions," he tweeted. "Headed home for a new start." And the winner of the 2012 NBA Championship was? The Miami Heat.

FERAL FRIGHT

In 1985, while a pitcher for the Houston Astros, superstar Nolan Ryan made a bad decision off the field. And it cost him on the field. During a drive in the country, Ryan spotted a dog pen that housed three coyote puppies. Without thinking, he reached in to pet the adorable pups. One skittish pup took a bite out of the Texas All-Star, who had to miss his next start for the Astros to undergo painful rabies treatments.

NOTHING TO SNEEZE AT

MLB right fielder and home run favorite Sammy Sosa was sitting in the Cubs dugout in San Diego talking to reporters in May of 2004 when he sneezed…violently. Then he sneezed again. And again. And again. Believe it or not, sneezes can travel through a person's body at speeds of up to 100 miles per hour. By the time Sosa's sneezing fit ended, he had sprained the ligaments in his lower back. It was enough to put him on the disabled list for a few games. Embarrassing? "It would have been better if I had run into the wall or had a fight with somebody," Sosa told reporters.

A snake cannot slither on glass.

HEAD-BUTT HOSPITAL

In 1997, Redskins quarterback Gus Frerotte was pumped after scoring a touchdown. But he didn't do an end-zone dance or kneel for a quick "thank you" prayer. He ran, full speed, at the nearest stadium wall, spiked the ball against it, and then slammed his helmeted head right into it. Bad idea. An ambulance had to rush Frerotte to the hospital, where he was diagnosed with a concussion and a badly strained neck. The Redskins had to finish the game with another quarterback.

IRONING IT OUT

Atlanta Braves Hall-of-Famer John Smoltz swears the reporter got it wrong. But according to the *Atlanta Journal Constitution*, Smoltz suffered five inch-long burns on his right chest in 1990 when he tried to iron his shirt—while he was wearing it. The article quoted Smoltz as saying, "I couldn't believe it. I've done it five or six times and never had that happen."

BASEBALL WITH BITE

To look more menacing, Boston Red Sox pitcher Clarence Blethen liked to take out his false teeth and slip them into his hip pocket. During a 1923 game, he seems to have forgotten they were there. When it came time to bat, he made a solid hit. He ran to first, touched the base, and kept running. Then he slid, feet first into second, and…his teeth bit him in the butt.

SMELL YA LATER!

Sure, these jokes and riddles stink. But don't let that stop you from laughing.

Teacher: Sam, please spell "new."
Sam: N-e-w.
Teacher: Very good. Now spell "canoe."
Sam: K-n-e-w.

Diner: Do you think lobsters are healthy?
Waiter: They must be. They never complain.

Teacher: How do you spell Mississippi?
Student: The river, or the state?

Farmer: Folks in the country go to bed with the chickens.
City Slicker: Well, in town we'd rather sleep in our own beds.

Harry: If you want to find your dog, you should put an ad in the paper.
Larry: Don't be silly. My dog can't read!

First Dragon: Am I late for dinner?
Second Dragon: Yes. Everyone's eaten.

Cat: What smells the most in a garbage dump?
Rat: The nose.

Mom: Doctor! The baby swallowed a pen. What should I do?
Doctor: Use a pencil.

Big Sister: We can't keep horses in the house. Think of the smell!
Little Brother: The horses will get used to it

More than 125 million yards of fabric have been used to make Barbie clothes.

TIME MACHINES

Real-life time machines? Why not?

THE TIPLER TIME MACHINE

Frank Tipler has been fascinated with time travel since he was five years old. In 1974, he designed a time machine that he hoped would work in real life. In his design, a person would take off in a spaceship and arrive at a cylinder rotating in space. Tipler believed that if the cylinder had enough mass and was rotating fast enough, it would work like an artificial black hole and have the power to warp time. After orbiting the cylinder the spaceship would go backward in time and it would be the past when the ship returned to Earth. The design had a few problems: to generate a black hole, the cylinder would have to be *infinitely* long. Once within the vortex created by the fake black hole, your ship would not be able to generate enough velocity to escape. So...you'd be stuck there. But not for long: Your ship would be crushed, and you'd be dead.

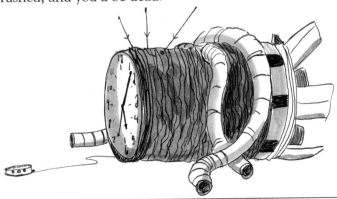

Non-island Rhode Island got the name because it was rich with red clay...

THE MALLETT LASER LOOP

Ronald Mallett, a professor at the University of
Connecticut, has dreamed of building a time machine
since he was 10. That's when his father died of a
heart attack. If he could travel back in time—Mallett
decided—he could warn his father to stop smoking.
Mallett's time-machine design uses light energy (four
laser beams) to warp space and time. It takes a Ph.D.
to understand the details, but according to Mallett, the
beams could swirl space and time like "a spoon stirring
milk into coffee." Mallett says he'll need about ten years
in the lab to make his time-travel dream real.

THE HAWKING WORMHOLE

"Wormholes are all around us, only they're too small
to see," says physicist Stephen Hawking. He describes
wormholes as "tiny crevices, wrinkles, and voids" in the
universe that connect separate areas of space and time.
If scientists could learn to devise a machine that would
make a wormhole bigger—say, the right size for a human
to pass through—it might make a handy time machine.
Unfortunately, right now, Hawking doesn't know how
to do that. What he does know? What he'd do with a
wormhole time machine if he had one: "If I had a time
machine, I'd visit Marilyn Monroe in her prime or drop
in on Galileo as he turned his telescope to the heavens."

*   *   *

"The strongest of all warriors are these two—Time and
Patience."

—Leo Tolstoy

SURVIVOR!

What would you do if you'd survived a killer virus only to discover that you couldn't walk? Here's what one kid did.

A CRIPPLING DISEASE

Thanks to vaccinations, polio is a rare disease today. But in 1913, when Mexican painter Frida Kahlo was six years old, many children caught the disease. Polio strikes children far more often than adults. Here's why: The virus lives in human guts and leaves the body through feces (poop). Kids are less likely to wash their hands after going to the bathroom. If they have the virus and then touch something that ends up in someone's else's mouth (food or water, for example) they spread the virus. Polio can cripple, paralyze, or even kill its victims. At its peak, the virus paralyzed and killed more than half a million people *every year*.

THE DOOR TO HEALING

When Frida caught the virus, the muscles in her right leg stopped working. She had to stay home from school for nine months. Because the disease is contagious, her friends couldn't visit. She was lonely and bored. So Frida used her imagination. She fogged the window with her breath and drew a misty door that led to a make-believe world. When she wanted to leave her bed and the dead weight of her paralyzed leg behind, she pictured herself flying through that door. In the world beyond the door, Frida could play and dance and enjoy life with secret friends. The pictures she painted in her mind got her through the illness. And they taught her to harness the creative power of the imagination.

SOCKS AND SOCCER

Polio left Frida's right leg thin, weak, and shorter than her other leg. Kids at school called her "Frida Peg Leg." The teasing bothered her so much that she wore extra socks to hide her thin leg. Other kids might have let the taunts stop them from returning to a normal playful life. Not Frida. She turned to sports to make her leg stronger.

Soccer, boxing, and wrestling weren't exactly for girls back then. But Frida loved them. Her father encouraged her to play. Though she would always walk with a limp, she would also swim, roller-skate, bicycle, and even play pranks at school, like riding a donkey down the hall. (Caution: We don't even want to *think* about what would happen if you decided to follow Frida's example.)

THE PAIN IN PAINTING

Play helped Frida leave polio behind, but life had something worse in store. During her senior year, Frida was riding a bus home from school. As the bus rounded a corner, a trolley slammed into it. Frida was thrown from the bus and ended up with a metal rail driven through her body. At the hospital, doctors found fractures to her spine, collarbone, and ribs; a shattered pelvis; and shoulder and foot injuries. This time, Frida spent over a year in bed. To escape the boredom, she began to paint.

Her mother bought a special easel so that she could paint while lying down. Her father gave her his own box of paints and brushes—she'd had her eye on the box for years. The accident that caused Frida terrible pain for the rest of her life also made her one of the world's greatest painters. "I've done my paintings well," Frida once told a friend. "Not quickly, but patiently. And they have a message of pain in them."

In 1953, Frida Kahlo had her first solo exhibition in Mexico. "It is impossible to separate the life and work of this extraordinary person," wrote one art critic. "Her paintings are her biography." Health challenges haunted Frida's entire life, but the lessons she learned as a child helped her to survive and to become one of the most successful painters of her time.

FAST FACTS ABOUT FRIDA'S ART

• Frida Kahlo was the first Mexican artist to have a painting hung in France's famous Louvre art museum.

• She was the first artist to have a painting sell for more than $1 million.

• More than half a century after her death, Kahlo's paintings still sell for more than those of any other female artist.

Discover other famous people who survived polio, on page 164.

Rabbits communicate through foot-thumping.

ANGLING FOR A MATE

Next time you think you have it bad, consider the fate of the male deep-sea angler fish.

The deep-sea angler fish lives about 3,000 feet below the surface of the world's oceans. There is almost no light that deep, so how does the angler catch a meal? For the female, it's easy: She has a piece of dorsal spine that sticks above her mouth like a fishing pole. (Yep. That's what gave the fish its name.) The "pole" is tipped with a bit of flesh that glows in the dark. It makes a perfect lure for drawing prey into her very toothy jaws.

Things aren't so easy for the male. When a male matures, its digestive system stops working. It has to find another way to get food—or starve. So the male goes looking for a female. He's a little guy (about the size of a pinky finger). She's bigger (between 8 inches and 3.3 feet long). The male uses his hook-like teeth to bite into the female. Then he releases an enzyme that dissolves the female's skin *and* his own mouth. Over time he "dissolves" into the female. He loses his eyes and all his internal organs (other than his reproductive organs), and in return he gets nourishment from the female's bloodstream. A female angler fish can carry up to 6 males. When she is ready to spawn, she has her choice of mates.

WILD WEATHER TALES

These weather misadventures are almost too weird to believe. But they're true!

THE HAND OF GOD

Members of the Methodist church in the small coastal community of Swan Quarter, North Carolina, knew all about the dangers of high tides and swollen creeks. That's why they didn't want to build their new sanctuary on Oyster Creek Road. When storms howled in from the nearby Atlantic, the creek was prone to flooding. Church members wanted to buy a vacant lot a few blocks away from the creek. The location seemed much safer. But the lot's owners wouldn't sell. The church had to settle for a lot on Oyster Creek Road after all. On September 16, 1876, they dedicated the church building and then asked for God's blessing on it.

Three days later, flood waters raged through Swan Quarter. Many buildings were damaged or uprooted. The new Methodist church was ripped from its foundation. It floated down the flooded street and around the corner, where it bumped into the general store. The building took a sharp right, then a left before it settled—safely—in a new location: the lot church members had originally hoped to buy.

Who could argue with a miracle? The land's owners deeded the lot to the church. And the name of the church was changed. It's now called The Church Moved by the Hand of God.

RIDE 'EM, COWGIRL!

In 1955, nine-year-old Sharon Weron was riding her horse home from a neighbor's house in Bowdle, South Dakota. The day was sticky. The air thick and hard to breathe: just right for a tornado. Suddenly, Sharon came face-to-face with a powerful twister. There was no way to outrun the storm. Sharon—and her horse—were lifted into the air.

Sharon's mother, who had been driving along behind her daughter, watched in horror. "The horse looked like a roll of wire," she said, "and seemed to be going in circles." Girl and horse spun in midair, soared over three fences, and traveled more than 1,000 feet before they hit ground again...safe and sound.

DISASTER DOGS

On April 27, 2011, a tornado blasted through Madison, Alabama, turning the Chambless home to rubble. The couple, Chase and Calen Chambless, survived. But they lost almost everything. Worst of all, their dogs, Bella, a seven-year-old West Highland terrier, and Kiaha, a three-year-old Australian shepherd, were missing.

The devastated couple posted signs and hoped for the best. Two days later, Bella was found on the opposite side of the neighborhood under a pile of debris. Her eyes were swollen shut and she couldn't see. She was dirty and covered in insulation, but she was alive.

But where was Kiaha? Days went by without any sign of the Australian shepherd. The couple placed ads in the paper, posted on Facebook, and ran radio appeals for the missing dog. And they asked all their friends and neighbors to watch for Kiaha.

Seven days after the tornado, Calen got a phone call. A tattered dog had been spotted sitting in what used to be the front yard of the Chambless home. "What was the name of your missing dog?" asked the caller. When Calen told her, she shouted out the name: "Kiaha!" The dog whimpered like she was crying.

"We may not have anything but the clothes on our backs," said Calen, "but at least we have our family, our whole family."

WHAT THE WHAT?

The U.S. has a lot of weird idioms. They're expressions that don't mean what they seem to mean, like "It's raining cats and dogs." Looks like other countries have them, too.

To Armenians "Stop ironing my head" means "quit bothering me."

To Germans "To talk a pork chop on someone's knee" means talking too much.

In Peru "Because of pure green peas" means "for no good reason."

To Japanese "To move the wings of one's nose incessantly" means to brag about something.

To Serbians "Ripping the clouds with your nose" means acting vain.

In Spain "Go fry asparagus" means the same thing as "Go fly a kite" means in the U.S.

When Germans say "I'll squeeze my thumbs for you," they're wishing you good luck.

To Russians "I'm not hanging noodles on your ears" means "I'm not tricking you."

MEET SNAKE-GIRL

Grab hold of one foot. Lean forward and tip your head down. Can you put your foot behind your head? No? Then read on!

TWIST 'ER! Okay, here's another one. Get down on all fours and form a bridge with your body. Now, lift your back left foot and move it forward so that your foot is tucked under your chin. Are you there yet? Neither are we. But if you could do it, you would have some idea of what it's like to be Nokulunga Buthelezi of South Africa.

Known as "Lunga" to her friends and "Snake-Girl" to the rest of the world, Nokulunga is a contortionist—an entertainer who can twist and bend her body into strange and unnatural positions. Being a human Gumby comes naturally to Lunga. Even as a toddler, she could bend and twist her body into positions that would tear muscles and break bones in other people. In fact, she was so flexible that her parents worried about her.

"I slept with my legs behind my head and my hands

behind my back," she said. "My mom thought there was something wrong with me."

Some contortionists are "shockers" and have to dislocate their own joints to contort their bodies. Lunga is an "artistic contortionist." All of her moves come naturally. Her family believes she inherited "snake genes" from her great-grandmother.

WHAT STRETCHY LIMBS YOU HAVE

The young Snake-Girl went to elementary school in Johannesburg, South Africa. She loved performing for her teachers and classmates. That's exactly what she was doing when a circus talent scout spotted her. Lunga was flexible enough to do an entire act, and she loved performing. So at age nine, she left her home and family to perform with the traveling circus. In her spare time, Lunga polished elephants' toenails and made friends with tigers. It was an exciting life, but she missed South Africa.

When Lunga turned 16, she starred in a touring circus called *Afrika! Afrika!* The show celebrated the talents, dancing, music, and art of the African continent. Since she missed out on having a "normal" childhood in South Africa, Lunga really enjoyed celebrating home through her art. Now a young adult, Lunga still performs all over the world. Dressed in a shimmery snakeskin-like body suit, she bends and twists herself into impossible positions. But how long can a contortionist's career last? "I have seen contortionists in their seventies," Lunga said. "So who knows?"

THAT'S SQUIRRELY

We've never seen a purple cow, and we never hope to see one. But this purple critter deserves a closer look.

YOU'VE GOT TO BE KIDDING

Connie and Percy Emert enjoy feeding the birds that visit their yard in Pennsylvania. But early in 2012, Mrs. Emert found a different sort of visitor at the feeder. "You're not going to believe it," she told her husband. "I saw a purple squirrel in the yard."

Mrs. Emert was right. Percy Emert didn't believe her. Because squirrels often steal seeds from their feeders, the Emerts keep a squirrel trap in their yard. If they trap a squirrel, Mr. Emert takes it to a safe place and sets it free. "I put a couple of peanuts inside the trap," he said.

Later that afternoon he found…a purple squirrel nibbling peanuts in the cage. Every hair on the squirrel's body was bright purple, as if it had been dyed. "Even the inside of its ears were purple," said Mr. Emert.

STICK 'EM UP!

The Emerts released the animal from the trap unharmed. But first they took fur samples from its purple tail. A state game warden came to the Emerts' house to collect any fur that had been left behind in the cage. No results

Geese can be trained to herd sheep.

have come from testing the samples yet, but there are lots of theories.

Henry Kacprzyk, a curator at the Pittsburgh Zoo, says that—except for the bright purple fur—the squirrel looks like an ordinary gray squirrel. Kacprzyk thinks the squirrel could have fallen into paint or dye. Or, he says, it might have been snacking on pokeberries before it headed to the Emerts' yard. The bright berries have been known to turn animals purple. One problem: The squirrel was spotted in February, when pokeberries are not in season.

TV meteorologist Henry Margusity said the squirrel could have fallen into a Porta-Potty. The blue chemicals used to treat human waste might have turned its fur purple. Or, since squirrels will chew on just about anything, it could have nibbled on a purple ink cartridge.

Our favorite theory: The squirrel robbed a bank, and the dye pack in the money bag exploded.

DON'T DRINK THE BACKWASH

Krish Pillai, an associate professor at Lock Haven University of Pennsylvania, had a more serious theory: "That color looks very much like Tyrian purple," he said. "It is a natural compound seen in mollusks (sea snails) and rarely found in land animals." He suggested that the squirrel might have too much bromide in its system from drinking bromide-laced water.

Where is the bromide coming from? In Pennsylvania, drillers are using water like dynamite to split apart shale (a kind of rock). The process is called "fracking." It releases natural gas trapped inside the shale, and the gas is then used to heat homes. When drillers blast water into shale, a mix of minerals and chemicals comes gushing up, too. Drillers call the bubbly brown stuff "flowback."

Bromide has been found in flowback. But that's only half the story. Water engineer Jeanne VanBriesen at Carnegie Mellon University discovered that when frack water goes through public water-treatment plants, it combines with the chlorine used for water treatment. And that creates a "potentially hazardous" compound.

CODE PURPLE

"I would raise the alarm," said Krish Pillai. If the squirrel found in the Emerts' yard turned purple after drinking water laced with bromide compounds, humans could be exposed, too. And purple hair would be the least of their worries. These chemicals could cause bladder cancer or other health problems.

The Emerts' find isn't the first purple squirrel that's been reported. In 2008, "Pete," the purple squirrel, lived on the grounds of Meoncross School in Stubbington, U.K. It's believed that Pete turned purple after chewing on a cartridge of purple ink. In 1997, a purple squirrel was photographed in Minnesota. Like the squirrel in the Emerts' yard, no one knows what natural (or unnatural) cause gave the animal its purple fur.

TOILET TEXTING

Wondering why your parents are spending so much time in the bathroom? Here's what a recent survey reveals.

• 75 percent of Americans say they use their cell phones while using the toilet. They not only chat and text with friends, some of them even conduct business meetings via their phones while enthroned.

• More than 90 percent of adults aged 28 to 35 use their mobile devices on the can.

• Sixteen percent of that group shop online while in the bathroom.

• 24 percent of adults will not even enter the stall unless they have their mobile device handy.

• About 63 percent answer the phone while on the john, and more than 40 percent have no qualms about calling someone else from there.

• Adults who have kids are more likely to use bathroom "privacy" for phone use than those who do not have kids.

• More than 90 percent of toilet phone users wash their hands when they're done, but 16 percent of cell phones have poop on them. (Hey, Dad? Sanitary wipes fix that.)

WHO NEEDS CLOTHES?

What has a thick neck, short legs, large feet, and hairy toes?
If your asnwer is "a hobbit," guess again.

A FACE ONLY MOM COULD LOVE

One of the weirdest animals on the planet lives in burrows beneath the sun-baked deserts of Eastern Africa: the naked mole rat. It is not really a mole. And it's not really a rat. But whoever named this odd little animal did get one thing right: it is as naked as a newborn baby.

Naked mole rats look like three-inch-long sausages with walrus tusks and skinny tails. Their skin is so baggy it looks two sizes too big. They have squinty little eyes, smooshed piglike noses, and giant teeth—two on the top and two on the bottom. People who see them at zoos often say: "They're so ugly, they're cute."

BUG OR BEAST?

Naked mole rats live in colonies, like termites, bees, and ants. "They're the most insect-like mammals I've ever seen," says biologist Dr. Paul W. Sherman. Colonies host up to 100 animals, and individuals put aside their needs so that the colony will survive. Workers, the smallest colony members, dig and shore up tunnels and look for

---

roots to harvest. Bigger members, both male and female, become soldiers. Only the biggest—the queen and one to three hulking mates—get to reproduce.

A naked mole rat will sacrifice its own life for the colony when needed. If a snake gets into a burrow, a single soldier will advance, seal up the tunnel behind itself, and let the snake eat it to save colony and queen. Why would an animal let itself be eaten? If you're a *Star Trek* fan, the answer is easy: because the needs of the many outweigh the needs of the few…or the one.

THE QUEEN RULES ALONE

As with termites and honeybees, the queen of a naked mole rat colony is huge compared to other colony members. And as she breeds, she becomes even bigger.

Despite bearing four or five litters of up to 27 pups per year (Yikes, 135 babies?), the queen has time to check up on colony members. She patrols the tunnels, watching as workers clear debris and soldiers guard against intruders. Her size helps her keep her subjects in line. She rules with brute force, pushing and shoving slackers to hurry their work.

SO HAPPY TOGETHER

Hundreds of naked mole rats living together in colonies may seem strange, but it makes sense when you consider their environment. Most naked mole rats live in the deserts of Kenya, Ethiopia, and Somalia. Droughts make food scarce. They survive on tubers that grow underground.

Easiest sounds for the human ear to notice, in order: *ah, aw, eh, ee, oo.*

Now, imagine a single three-inch-long animal wandering around a desert trying to find a tuber to eat. Impossible! Naked mole rats live in colonies because, by working together, the tiny animals can find and harvest enough food to survive.

Of course, that doesn't explain the whole "naked" thing. This does: The scorching desert sun can cook a mole rat faster than you can say "baked potato." So they live in tunnels underground. The temperature is a cozy 84°F there, year-round. With tunnels warm enough for a nudist colony, why would mole rats need fur or hair? They don't. If the temperature does cool off, they just snuggle together and transmit heat skin to skin.

WHERE'D YOU GET THOSE PEEPERS?

Because naked mole rats are almost always underground, they have teeny eyes that can only see shadows. Their pig-like noses are loaded with chemical sensors that make up for bad eyesight. They can recognize colony mates by smell, and they can follow their noses to food.

Even their baggy skin comes in handy. Since naked mole rats spend their lives scrabbling through narrow tunnels several feet below ground, loose skin makes it easy to wriggle over and around colony mates without getting scuffed up on tunnel walls.

Dr. Sherman says it took thousands of generations for naked mole rats to evolve charactistics that make them perfectly adapted to their environment. And, Sherman adds, "That's what makes them beautiful."

JUST THE NAKED (MOLE RAT) FACTS

• When passing in a tunnel, a smaller naked mole rat will crouch to let a larger one crawl over it.

• One naked mole rat will go outside to bask in the sun. When it has soaked up enough warmth, it comes inside to huddle with the others and share the heat, like "a living hot-water bottle."

• When debris drops into the tunnel, workers form a "bucket brigade," passing the dirt from rat to rat to sweep it outside.

• These odd little critters can run backward as easily as forward. A few whiskers on their heads and tails help them feel the way.

• Naked mole rats roll in the urine and feces of colony mates to coat themselves with a common odor.

• Naked mole rats produce 17 different sounds, as many as some primates.

• If the queen dies, other animals undergo a growth spurt, vying to replace her. Once a new queen wins the throne, the losers shrink back to their original sizes.

QUARTERBACK PROPS

These Super Bowl quarterbacks have something in common besides the Super Bowl! They've all ended up as cartoon versions of themselves on The Simpsons.

THE EPISODE: "Double, Double, Boy in Trouble"
STARRING: Joe Montana

Bart Simpson visits an ultra-rich family and notices what he thinks is a poster of Joe Montana on a wall. Then he discovers something: It really *is* Montana. "I'm the real deal," Montana says. "Every day that I stand here, the family donates a million dollars to Notre Dame." Notre Dame is the college Montana attended in real life. Also in real life, Montana won four Super Bowl titles, with his three MVP awards coming in numbers XVI, XIX, and XXIV.

THE EPISODE: "Bart Star"
STARRING: Joe Namath

Just after Bart says it will take a miracle for him to become a good quarterback, Joe Namath knocks on the Simpsons' door. Namath's car has broken down right outside their house. Bart can hardly believe his luck. He begs for football pointers, and Namath is just about to tell him the one thing he needs to know to become a great quarterback. But…Namath's wife gets the car started. "I've gotta run!" Joe says. "Remember what I told you!"

THE EPISODE: "Homer and Ned's Hail Mary Pass"
STARRING: Tom Brady
Brady was the MVP of Super Bowls XXXVI and XXXVIII. As a cartoon character, the New England Patriots quarterback saw a video clip of Homer doing a wildly ridiculous victory dance at a local carnival. Brady hires Homer to choreograph a victory dance for him. Homer's moves are such crowd pleasers, he's asked to choreograph the Super Bowl XXXIX halftime show.

THE EPISODE: "Sunday, Cruddy Sunday"
STARRING: Troy Aikman
Troy Aikman, the MVP of Super Bowl XXVII, played for the Dallas Cowboys. A shady travel agent offers Homer a free trip to the Super Bowl in Miami if he can fill a charter bus. But when the Springfield fans show up at the stadium, they find out their tickets are fakes. Things pick up when they find Troy Aikman running a caricature booth. Pictures of people riding in dune buggies line the booth's walls. When Ned sits for a caricature, Aikman says, "So, Ned, do you like dune buggies?" Ned tries to tell him no, but Aikman insists. "Sure you do!" he says. "Everyone likes dune buggies!" Then he draws Ned riding in a dune buggy, just as he's drawn everyone else who came to the booth.

THE EPISODE: "Treehouse of Horrors XVI"
STARRING: Terry Bradshaw
Terry Bradshaw led the Pittsburgh Steelers to four
Super Bowl titles, earning consecutive MVP awards
in numbers XIII and XIV. When his quarterback days
ended, Bradshaw began a career as a TV sports analyst
and co-host of Fox *NFL Sunday*. That experience
came in handy when Simpsons writers turned him
into a cartoon character. In the episode, Mr. Burns
lures Homer to his estate. Homer soon finds himself
to be an unwilling contestant in "The World Series of
Manslaughter." Bradshaw provides the play-by-play as
Mr. Burns hunts down his quarry.

THE EPISODE: "O Brother, Where Bart Thou?"
STARRING: Eli, Cooper, and Peyton Manning
Jealous of Maggie and Lisa's sisterly bond, Bart dreams
of having famous brothers: the Marx Brothers (Chico,
Harpo, and Groucho), the Mario Bros. (Mario and
Luigi), and the football-playing Manning brothers.
Eli and Peyton Manning, both Super Bowl MVPs,
toss a ball with their older brother, Cooper, who brags
about his glory days playing high school football. It's
bittersweet: In real life, Cooper was also on track for a
pro-football career but was sidelined by an injury. As
for voicing himself for *The Simpsons*? "It was fun," said
the real-life Cooper. "You can screw up as much as you
want. Just do your lines over and over for a couple of
takes, then throw some fake laughs in there."

ORPHANT ANNIE

You've probably heard of Little Orphan Annie. She got her start in this 1885 poem by James Whitcomb Riley.

Little Orphant Annie's come to our house to stay,
An' wash the cups and saucers up,
an' brush the crumbs away,
An' shoo the chickens off the porch,
an' dust the hearth and sweep,
An' make the fire, an' bake the bread,
an' earn her board-and-keep.
An' all us other children
when the supper things is done,
We set around the kitchen fire
an' has the mostest fun
A-list'nin' to the witch-tales
'at Annie tells about,
An' the Gobble-uns 'at gits you
Ef you
Don't
Watch
Out!

FOODIE ART!

*Mama John always said not to play with your food, but
Uncle John didn't always listen, so why should you?*

The **Project**: Jello-O Painting
Supplies: Jell-O (made up and chilled), thick
paper or poster board, paintbrush (optional)
What You Do: Mash the Jell-O with your fingers. Take
a handful and plop it onto your paper. Using your fingers
or a paintbrush, paint an abstract picture. Red Jell-O
works great for zombie attacks. Blue and green Jell-Os
are perfect for Godzilla and friends emerging from the sea.

The Project: Dyed stationery
Supplies: White paper; coffee, tea, juice, or Kool-Aid;
clothespins
What You Do: Pour a few cups of your choice beverage
into a large shallow baking dish. Slide a few pieces
of paper into the dish. Make sure they're completely
submerged, and leave them there for 30 minutes to an
hour. Carefully take out your colored sheets and use
clothespins to hang them to dry. *Voilà*—hand-dyed
stationery. Great for writing pen-pal letters, birthday
lists, or ransom notes for kidnapped Barbies.

The Project: PB&J Finger painting
Supplies: Paper, peanut butter (or other nut butter),
jelly or jam

What You Do: Dip your fingers in the peanut butter and use the spread as you would finger paint. Add colorful (and delicious) accents to your picture with jam or jelly. When you finish, you can let the "paint" dry or just go ahead and lick it off the paper. (You know you want to!)

The Project: Spice Fireworks
Supplies: Paper, glue, toothpick, sifter or sieve, ground spices
What You Do: Squeeze 5 to 10 dime-sized dots of glue onto your paper. Using a toothpick, spread each dot out in the pattern of an exploding firework. Finally, use a sifter or a sieve to sprinkle a small amount of a spice onto each firework. Before clipping the picture onto the fridge, let it dry completely. Sniffing your picture when you open the fridge? Optional.

The Project: Cracker Faces
Supplies: Townhouse-type crackers, sliced cheese, black olive slices, peas, chow mein noodles, sliced hard-boiled eggs, thin-sliced carrots
What You Do: Use any of the ingredients above (or whatever you have on hand) to make funny faces on crackers. Peas, or olive slices with peas in them, make silly eyes. Bits of olive, carrot, or chow mein noodles make great noses, mustaches, hair, smiles, or beards. Share your cracker art or chow down!

UFO WEATHER

*Have you ever seen a flying saucer? Are you sure?
According to scientists, more than 90 percent of UFO
sightings can be blamed on the weather.*

• Many of the UFOs people report seeing around the
world turn out to be...weather balloons.

• Weather conditions at night can sometimes make the
moon appear larger, smaller, or strangely colored. Five
percent of all reported UFO sightings are the moon.

• Then there's ball lightning: a small sphere of blinding
light that can appear much larger than it actually is and
be mistaken for a UFO. Meteorologists don't know what
causes ball lightning. So, technically, it's still a UFO.

• A lenticular cloud is thick, wavy, and saucer-shaped.
Noctilucent clouds are made of ice particles, so after the
Sun sets they have an eerie glow. Many UFOs turn out
to be lenticular or noctilucent clouds.

• A group of airline employees claimed they saw a
flying saucer at Chicago's O'Hare Airport in 2006. The
Federal Aviation Administration begged to differ. They
said the UFO was just airport lights reflecting off low
clouds. One official jokingly expressed sympathy for the
aliens. "To fly seven million light years to O'Hare and
then have to turn around and go home because your
gate was occupied is simply unacceptable," he said.

Florida is bigger than England.

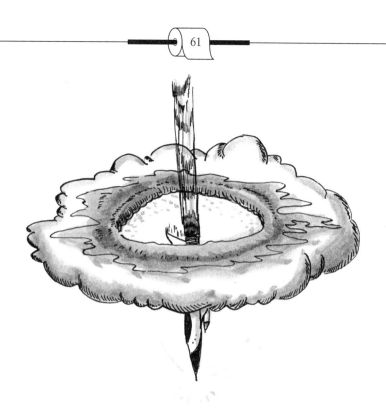

• Hole punch clouds are rare and are often mistaken for UFOs. What are they? Mostly mid- or high-altitude cirrus or cirro-stratus clouds that form above 20,000 feet in the atmosphere. The National Weather Service says that such clouds are composed of both ice crystals and super-cooled water droplets. If a plane punches through the clouds, it leaves an ice-rimmed hole that looks a lot like an UFO.

• Mirages can also trick people into thinking they've seen UFOs. When the air in a certain place is at several different density levels, as sometimes happens on a very hot day, light rays bend as they hit objects. That can cause a wavy shape that looks like a hovering UFO.

January 23rd is National Pie Day.

MEET WEENIE MAN

Here's how one famous cartoonist got started.

GO, WEENIES!
American cartoonist Garry Trudeau is best known for the comic strip *Doonesbury*. He started the strip while studying graphic design at Yale University, and it's been running for more than 40 years. But before he became a world-famous cartoonist, Trudeau was a small, shy, artsy kid who loved reading *Mad* magazine and acting.

At age 7, Trudeau started an acting company. He wrote plays and songs, made tickets and programs, and staged productions in his parents' basement. When he was 12, his parents divorced. The next year, he was on his way to St. Paul's, a boarding school in New Hampshire. Jocks ruled the in-crowd at his new school, and Trudeau got his share of teasing for his lack of athletic ability. And then...he created his first cartoon character: Weenie Man.

In 1965, during his senior year at St. Paul's, Trudeau did something that gained the jocks' respect. He drew Weenie Man on posters to help sell hot dogs at his school's football games. "He would solve vexing problems by literally tossing hot dogs at them," Trudeau said.

Weenie Man became the inspiration for Mike Doonesbury, a character who first showed up in 1968 in a strip called *Bull Tales*. Trudeau started drawing the strip for the *Yale Daily News* during his junior year at Yale. The comic featured Brian Dowling (B.D.), the football jock; Mark, the revolutionary; and Mike Doonesbury, the "little man on campus."

"For years I was a Mike Doonesbury myself," said Trudeau. "Always on the outside trying to get in." Not anymore! Trudeau made cartooning history when he won a Pulitzer Prize for editorial cartooning. He was the first cartoonist to ever receive one.

Meet more "Comic Geniuses" on page 212.

*   *   *

Q: How many pastry chefs does it take to make a pie?
A: 3.14

Q: What do you get when you divide a bovine's circumference by its diameter?
A: Cow pi

Q: Why do plants hate math jokes?
A: Because it gives them square roots.

Q: Why couldn't the circle button its pants?
A: It had too much pi.

OUTHOUSE LOGIC

Who knew using an outhouse required brain power?

There are four outhouses on the Winslow farm: a red one, a yellow one, a blue one, and a green one. The four Winslow children each have a favorite, and no one else ever uses it. Use these clues to figure out who uses which outhouse.

• Brady never uses his outhouse after dark.

• Marcia is the oldest kid.

• Luke plays his harmonica in the outhouse.

• Jade is two years younger than her twin brothers.

• The red outhouse is always in use at midnight.

• The youngest child uses the green outhouse.

• There's never any music in the blue outhouse.

• The red outhouse is used by one of the girls.

Find the secret to solving this kind of logic puzzle AND the answer on page 284.

It took Dr. Seuss a year and a half to write *The Cat in the Hat*.

What color is hippo sweat? Red.

ODD FROGS

Most of us have seen ordinary frogs croaking away at a pond or in the woods. But this page will probably be the closest you ever get to these rare amphibians.

THE ODD FROG: *Trichobatrachus robustus* (also called the Horror Frog)
WHERE IT CROAKS: Central Africa
FROGGY FACTS: This four-inch frog is known for its red hair. Wait...a frog with hair? Okay. It doesn't really have hair. But it does have red strands of skin dangling from its sides and back legs. It also has extendable claws (picture Wolverine in the X-Men movies). The frog's "claws" aren't fingernails or toenails. They're finger and toe *bones* that can break through the pads on the frog's digits to form weapons. When attacked, the Horror Frog thrusts these sharp bones into the skin of its enemies. As tough as they sound, Horror Frogs still have to watch out for the most dangerous predator: man. Hunters use long spears to kill the frogs so they won't get stabbed by those bony claws. Then—we're sorry to report—they roast the frogs and eat them.

THE ODD FROG: *Paedophryne amauensis*
WHERE IT CROAKS: Papua, New Guinea
FROGGY FACTS: Scientists discovered this copper-colored black-spotted frog in August of 2009. They soon realized it's the tiniest frog—in fact the tiniest vertebrate (animal with a spine)—in the whole world. At least, it's the smallest found so far. How small? The adults are only three-tenths of an inch long—the size of a common housefly. One of these tiny frogs can sit in the middle of a dime with plenty of room to spare. Searching for more tiny frogs is no easy task. Scientists listen carefully for their songs. But the male frog's mating call is so high it sounds like an insect chirping. It's so hard to spot them in the wild, scientists have started grabbing up gobs of leafy matter. They cart the leaves back to their labs and search carefully, hoping to spot a copper flash among the green.

THE ODD FROG: *Dyscophus antongilli* (also called the Tomato Frog)
WHERE IT CROAKS: Madagascar
FROGGY FACTS: Tomato Frogs look as red as the fruit they're named for, but that isn't what makes them truly weird. The fist-sized frogs have a seriously sticky defense mechanism. Their bright-red color warns most predators away. But if a hungry snake can't resist taking a bite, it ends up with a mouth full of white goo that looks and acts just like school glue. The snake lets go of the frog to get the gunk out of its mouth, but its teeth and mouth will stay gummed up for days.

Your brain holds between 1 and 7 million megabytes (1 to 7 terabytes) of data.

KIDS INCORPORATED

Nobody asks these kids what they want to be when they grow up. Why? Because they're already in business.

HARLI JORDEAN

When he was six, Harli Jordean loved marbles so much he slept with them under his pillow. He also took them with him to school to trade. Big mistake: Older kids snatched his collection. So Harli asked his mom to help him buy a new supply on the Internet. "His obsession was so big, we started calling him the Marble King," said his mother.

Finding marbles online wasn't easy. That gave Harli an idea: start an online marble store of his own. His mom helped him create a website, and orders flooded in. Today, nine-year-old Harli sells marbles by the hundreds. And he pockets thousands of dollars every year. Orders are so brisk, he's hired his mother and two older brothers to help handle the demand.

LEANNA ARCHER

The one thing people always noticed about 9-year-old Leanna Archer was her hair. Leanna used a hair pomade from a secret recipe passed down from her Haitian great-grandmother. She got so many compliments from friends, she made batches to share with them. Orders started pouring in—people wanted to *buy* her hair products. Leanna started a business in her basement, and at age 13 she became the youngest CEO ever to ring the opening bell for the NASDAQ stock market. Every school day, after finishing her homework, Leanna packs boxes to fill orders from her website. On weekends, her parents help out. All that work pays off: 16-year-old Leanna pockets $100,000 per year.

KENT MELVILLE

Three things set ten-year-old Kent Melville apart from the crowd: 1) Kent has autism, 2) he owns a successful soft drink company, and 3) he's ten years old. How'd he get started? With a lemonade stand.

In the summer of 2010, Kent wanted to earn some money. His parents let him start a lemonade stand at their Vermont home. His stand did very, very well, and Kent asked his parents if he could start a soft drink company. His father advised him to wait a few years.

"There are lots of other kids with autism," Kent said. "I want to be able to help them get some of the things they want with the money we earn. Can't we start now?" His dad couldn't say no to that. Kent's Soda Company sells lemonade (of course), but also root beer and raspberry-lime, orange, and cream sodas. Part of the profits go to clubs, camps, and programs for kids with autism all over the country.

GIRLS IN SPORTS PART I

These days, girls play almost all sports boys play. But it wasn't always so. Here are a few of the benchmarks that won (or almost lost) girls the right to be jocks.

• **396 B.C.** The city state of Sparta stood out in the Greek world. For one thing, Spartan girls went out for the same sports as boys. They even played sports wearing few (or no) clothes…just like the boys. Spartan princess Kyniska, daughter of King Archidamus II, was the first woman to win an Olympic event—a four-horse chariot race. Of course, the victor's crown went to the chariot's owner, not to its driver. (Which was why the princess was allowed to compete in the all-male games.)

• **AD 1804.** British rider Alicia Meynell was the first female jockey. Dressed in a leopard-print dress and waistcoat, she competed in a four-mile race on a friend's horse, Vingarillo. Meynell lost, but just barely.

• **1837.** Author Donald Walker's book *Exercise for Ladies* warns women against horseback riding, claiming it deforms the lower half of their bodies.

• **1873.** Ten girls compete in a 1-mile swimming race in the Harlem River. The prize? A silk dress worth $175.

A horse breathes through its mouth only when it is panicked.

- **1875.** The "Blondes" take on the "Brunettes" in Springfield, Illinois, in a match billed as "the first game of baseball ever played in public for gate money between feminine ball-tossers."

- **1876.** Shocked observers watch Mary Marshall beat Peter Van Ness in a speed-walking match in New York City—Mary took Peter in the best two out of three.

- **1876.** Nell Saunders defeats Rose Harland in the first U.S. women's boxing match and wins…a silver butter dish.

- **1891.** Fourteen-year-old Beatrice von Dressden of Buffalo, New York, is one of the first females to make a parachute jump from a hot-air balloon.

- **1895.** Annie Smith Peck climbs to the top of the Matterhorn. With a summit at 14,692 feet, it's one of the highest peaks in the Swiss Alps. Peck climbed wearing a pair of knickerbockers (short pants) with thick leggings, both of which she sewed by hand. (The press went nuts over those knickerbockers.)

More benchmarks on page 262.

Dirty snow melts faster than clean snow.

SALTED EARTHWORMS

At long last, the answer to which unusual meats really taste like chicken.

• Some people say **alligator meat** tastes a bit like lobster, but others think "old, muddy fish" is more on target. We've also heard that alligator tastes like veal or rabbit. And some say it tastes like rattlesnake. The tail meat is said to be the most tender part. It's expensive: five pounds of all-white tail meat costs a whopping $96 on Amazon.com. Despite the price, Americans eat more than a million pounds of gator every year.

• **Rattlesnake** has a fishy texture, and some compare it to crab. In the American Southwest where the snakes tend to be large, many people eat them.

• A **python** is usually quite a bit larger than a rattlesnake, so its meat tends to be tougher. The taste of its meat is said to be a gamey cross between scallops and chicken. People in many cultures eat snakes, particularly in Asian countries.

• We've heard that **rat meat** is "a little like pork," but rattier. Actually, rats taste a lot like whatever they've been eating. A country rat prefers grains, fruit, and seeds. But a city rat will eat whatever it can find, including smaller rodents like mice.

• We haven't tried them, but dried **salted earthworms** are supposed to taste like beef jerky. Earthworms used to be a common food in China. The 1848 edition of a book by a French naval officer described a meal he was offered in China. The first course: "salted earth-worms, prepared and dried, but so cut up that I fortunately did not know what they were until I had swallowed them." The Chinese have also been known to eat earthworm soup to cure a fever. (And you thought chicken soup was hard to keep down when you're sick.)

• Insects are eaten in many cultures. **Roasted crickets** taste like nuts, and some **fried caterpillars** taste like bacon. Certain **termites** have a lemony bacon flavor.

• There are **giant spiders** in New Guinea that are said to taste like peanut butter. (But can you spread them on toast?)

• Australian **honey ants** are said to be as sweet as their name. They store a sugary liquid that gives them their flavor, though it's more like molasses than honey. They're a traditional food of Australia's Aboriginal people. To eat one, you simply pick it up by the head and bite off the belly.

* * *

Dad: Why do I need goggles to look at your report card?
Kid: Because my grades are all under C.

BEASTS OF THE DEEP

Earth's surface has its own collection of freaks and geeks (the platypus, for example). But the true weirdos live deep underwater, where they regularly terrorize their aquatic friends and neighbors.

THE ABOMINABLE CRUSTACEAN

Humans like to think they know all there is to know about the planet. But every so often we discover something that throws us for a loop. That happened in 2006, when scientists were trolling more than a mile deep in the southeastern Pacific Ocean. They came across the yeti crab, a blind albino crustacean with claws so furry they look like a shag rug. The fur has a purpose: catching bacteria, the yeti crab's favorite food. Yeti is so strange, scientists classified him in his very own family and genus, *Kiwaidae kiwa*.

RAT, DOG, ELEPHANT—OR FISH?

The chimaera is a deep-sea creature with both fins and wings. It glides along the mud more than a mile deep in northern oceans around the world. The name *chimaera* is tough to read (ki-meer-rah). So it's a good thing the fish has a catchy collection of nicknames: "rat-fish," "dog-fish," "elephant-fish," and the especially fetching "elongated carrot with wings," given to it by a British biologist. A chimaera's looks vary—some species have unbelievably long snouts with "electroreceptive" pores. As they wave their snouts across the ocean floor, they can "see" electric fields given off by other sea creatures. Other species boast dead white eyes and venomous spines. Some say that artists who want to represent nightmares and other demons of darkness should hire chimaeras as models.

YOU'VE GOT SOMETHING IN YOUR TEETH

Another prime candidate for "Most Hideous Thing in the Ocean" is the viperfish. It's a black, eel-like swimmer with vacant eyes and a jaw that appears unhinged. But its teeth are the stars of the show. Like overgrown fingernails, they extend out of the fish's lower jaw, all the way up to eye level. When a viperfish spots a tasty morsel, it pounces like a snake and impales the food with its teeth. Viperfish roam depths of almost two miles in the Mediterranean sea and in the Atlantic, Pacific, and Indian oceans.

TUNE IN TO TV

*Before you grab the remote to watch one of your favorite
200 channels, here's a look at television's humble beginnings.*

1930s: TV? Forget about it. In the 1930s, gas cost 10
cents a gallon. Kids played with electric trains. And
radio—not TV—was America's #1 source of family
entertainment. During the Great Depression a lot of
people were out of work. A "big night out" for a family
wasn't a night out at all. Families gathered around radios
to listen to their favorite programs. Cost of that radio?
Between $14.65 and $370.65.

1940s: Clark Gable starred in *Gone with the Wind*
(released in late 1939) on the big screen. The
movie took advantage of the latest developments in
Technicolor® technology for a bigger color palette than
moviegoers had ever seen. As for TV—the picture on
a TV screen was strictly black-and-white. That didn't
stop Motorola ads from pitching its TV sets as being for
viewers "who have awaited television perfection." Those
"perfect" TV sets cost $279, nearly 10 percent of an
average family's yearly income of $3,000. By the end of
the 1940's, about 4 million households had a TV set.

1950s: A new car cost $1,500. Mr. Potato Head was all
the rage with kids. And, by 1953, 20 million people had
purchased TV sets. With its giant 27-inch screen, the

set made by Stewart-Warner Electric had a picture that was "bigger than life size." The price? Only $199.

1960s: Gas was 25 cents a gallon and talking Barbie asked girls if they'd like to go shopping. It was the decade of the "two-TV family." Motorola offered a real bargain: For only $139, a family could buy a 19-inch black-and-white TV. In 1967, prices soared again. Color TV had arrived. A "personal size" color set cost $329.95.

1970s: Kids listened to music on 8-track tape players. Truckers used CB radios to warn each other about "bear traps" (police sitting behind billboards with radar guns). And Panasonic promised to make horror movies more horrible than ever with its Quintrix II color picture tube. In 1972, Magnavox released the first home video game console: the Odyssey. Early video games had something in common with the first big-screen films: no sound.

1980s: Communism collapsed. The first "personal computers" debuted. One popular toy? A talking doll based on a friendly furry space alien named Alf who starred in a hit TV series. In other TV news: Sony tried to get sports fans to spend big bucks on big TVs with its giant 51-inch Videoscope. Programming on the Videoscope, Sony said, "was a whole new ball game." Rock and roll fans had something new, too: a brand new channel called MTV. Turns out, music fans bought big TVs as often as jocks did.

ILLEGAL NOSE-PICKING!

Can you really be arrested for picking your nose in Israel?

NOSE NEWS IS GOOD NEWS

The no nose-picking rule started with a rumor. An Israeli newpaper reported that Rabbi Ovadia Yosef had said nose-picking on the Sabbath was forbidden. Why? Because tiny hairs inside the nostrils might also be pulled out. (Ouch!) Those of the Jewish faith are not allowed to trim their hair or nails on the Sabbath. So accidental nose-hair plucking could indeed be a no-no. Rabbi Yosef is one of a select group of rabbis who answer questions—serious or silly—about applying Jewish law to daily life. Further investigation revealed that Yosef had actually ruled that nose-picking on the Sabbath was OK. (But it's snot recommended.)

Game show lingo: a contestant who gets nervous and freezes...

Believe it or not, these laws are real:

• In **Singapore**, it's illegal to pee in an elevator.

• It's against the law to leave home in **Thailand** without wearing underwear.

• You need a license to buy a TV in **Norway**.

• In **Russia**, the law prohibits brushing your teeth more than twice a day.

• Apartment dwellers in **Switzerland** aren't allowed to flush a toilet after 10 p.m.

• Taxi cabs in **Australia** are required to carry a bale of hay in the trunk.

• It's illegal to water your lawn in Nova Scotia, **Canada**, when it's raining.

• In **France**, you are not permitted to name a pig Napoleon.

• Disc jockeys in **Argentina** are required to play as many tango records as all other types of music combined.

• Bears are not permitted on the beach in **Israel**, but...

• ...throwing Brussels sprouts at tourists is perfectly legal for **Belgians**.

* * *

Smell-O-Fact: An American company once tried to buy The Beatles' bathwater. Why? To bottle it and sell it to fans. The Fab Four said no thanks.

OFF THEIR DUFFS

These famous writers didn't just work out their typing fingers. They flexed other muscles, too.

Before writing **The Red Badge of Courage...** Stephen Crane was a catcher on the Syracuse University baseball team. He didn't graduate, though. In fact, he flunked out of three different colleges before finding success as a writer.

Before writing *Charlie and the Chocolate Factory*... Roald Dahl played soccer, boxed in his school's heavyweight division, and captained the school's squash team (squash, as in the game similar to racquetball, not the vegetable). Dahl went on to flex his muscles as a fighter pilot for the British Royal Air Force during WWII... until he got lost flying his plane to Egypt and crash-landed in the Libyan desert.

Before winning the Newbery Medal for *Maniac Magee*... Jerry Spinelli played a lot of Little League baseball. He started playing at age 11, and until age 16 he was sure he'd grow up to be a Major League shortstop. What happened at age 16? A local newspaper published his poem about a big win by his school's football team. In school the next day, everyone told him how much they loved the poem: teachers, coaches...and girls. It was a career-changing moment.

Wearing headphones for an hour increases the bacteria in your ears by 700 times.

Before *The Jungle Book*...author Rudyard Kipling enjoyed golf so much that he played it all winter. He's credited with inventing the game of snow golf while living in Vermont. He painted the golf balls red and made cups out of tin cans placed in the snow.

Before becoming a world-famous poet... Lord Byron earned his strokes as an excellent swimmer. His club foot sometimes left him embarrassed on land, but it didn't slow him down in the water. In 1810, he swam across a choppy three-mile stretch of water between Europe and Asia that connects the Aegean Sea with the Black Sea. He wrote about the swim in a famous poem, "Written After Swimming from Sestos to Abydos." And that made his feat the first *recorded* open-water swim of modern times. A race is held there every year in honor of Lord Byron's swim.

Before *I Know Why the Caged Bird Sings*...Maya Angelou was a teen who loved to dance. She even won a scholarship to study dance at San Francisco's Labor School. At age 14, Angelou sidestepped out of school into a job as San Francisco's first African-American female cable-car conductor. But within a few years she was back to dancing. She studied modern dance with Martha Graham and danced with Alvin Ailey on TV variety shows. And then, in 1968, Dr. Martin Luther King, Jr., was assassinated. It happened on her birthday, and Angelou was heartbroken. She stopped dancing to write her first novel, *I Know Why the Caged Bird Sings*.

A lemon can power a light bulb.

DON'T POO-POO THESE POOCHES

Think dogs can't really be "man's best friend"? Then you haven't met these daring do-gooders.

THE POOCH: Ted, a toy poodle
THE DARING DO: In September of 2011, firefighters responded to a call in West Jordan, Utah. They found a house in flames with smoke pouring from the windows. They also found...Ted.

"Two of our paramedics had gone inside to search the structure," said Fire Battalion Chief Reed Sharman. "When they opened the door, there was the dog."

When the paramedics tried to grab the tiny poodle, he ran downstairs. At the first landing, Ted stopped and looked back at the paramedics. He waited for them to follow, and then he ran down to the next landing. Each time the paramedics got close, the poodle led them a little further into the basement. That's where they found Ted's owner, a 19-year-old man who had been overcome by smoke inhalation.

THE POOCH: Kilo, the pit bull
THE DARING DO: On April 4, 2012, a FedEx delivery man knocked on the door of Kevin Becker's New York City apartment. Becker didn't think twice

about opening the door. But Kilo, his faithful 12-year-old pit bull wasn't so trusting. As Becker opened the door, Kilo rushed to his side. It wasn't the FedEx man after all. It was a robber dressed as a delivery man.

As the man tried to force his way inside, Kilo pushed his head out the door to keep him out. "The stranger shot him," Becker said. "Then the coward ran off." The bullet bounced off Kilo's skull and exited through his neck. Would the hero pit bull pull through?

Yes! "This is one in a million," said Dr. Greg Panarello, the veterinarian who treated Kilo. "He's very lucky."

THE POOCH: La China, a stray mutt

THE DARING DO: A 14-year-old girl in Argentina gave birth to a baby. Then the frightened young mother abandoned her newborn in a pile of trash. La China, a stray dog with a litter of six puppies, stepped in.

Police believe the dog probably heard the baby crying, and her motherly instincts kicked in. Cheena dragged the baby from the trash heap, wrapped her body around the tiny baby, and warmed it alongside her pups. Sometime later, a human neighbor heard the baby's cries and called police to investigate.

"She took the baby like a puppy and preserved it," police said. "The doctors told us if she hadn't done this, the baby would have died."

Worldwide ratio of humans to chickens: 1:1.

BE A MIND READER!

Follow these five easy steps and convince your friends that you can read their minds.

1. Find an accomplice. (*Mwa-ha-ha!*) Teach your accomplice the trick before performing it in public.

2. Lay eight cards of the same suit on a table. (You should end up with an ace and the number cards 2 to 8. Consider the ace to be a 1.)

3. Spread the eight cards on a table in front of a group. Then leave the room.

4. The accomplice lets the group choose a card by turning it over so everyone can see it. The accomplice turns the card facedown and calls you back to the room.

5. When you come in, ask the group to picture the card in their minds. Then amaze everyone by correctly identifying the card.

How it works: The key to this trick is in how the accomplice calls you back into the room. Let's say that your name is Sam. If the accomplice says, "OK, Sam," then you know the group picked the 2 card. If he says, "Come back in now," they chose the 4 card. How do you know that? The number of words your accomplice uses to call you back indicates the number of the chosen card. Just be sure your accomplice knows how to count!

The piece of your nose between your nostrils is called the *columella*.

IMPOSSIBLE!

A few infamous examples of how wrong experts can be.

"There is practically no chance communications space satellites will be used to provide better telephone, telegraph, television, or radio service inside the U.S."

—FCC Commissioner T. Craven, 1961

"That is the biggest fool thing we have ever done. The atomic bomb will never go off, and I speak as an expert in explosives."

—Admiral William Leahy, 1944

"Heavier-than-air flying machines are impossible."

—British Physicist, Lord Kelvin, 1895

"The idea that the cavalry will be replaced by these iron coaches is absurd. It is a little short of treasonous."

—British Field Marshal Haig, at a tank demonstration, 1916

"The abdomen, the chest, and the brain will forever be shut from the intrusion of the wise and humane surgeon."

—John Eric Erickson, surgeon to Queen Victoria, 1873

"Rail travel at high speeds is not possible because passengers, unable to breathe, would die of asphyxia."

—Professor Dionysius Lardner, London, 1830s

WALRUS STAMPEDE

Herds of huge marine animals are running for their lives.
But it may be too late.

SHORE IS HOT

In 2007, more than 500 walruses were trampled to death in a stampede in Russia. In 2009, 131 were trampled near Anchorage, Alaska. What is driving herds of marine mammals to run for their lives? "Global warming," says Anatoly Kochnev, a marine biologist at Russia's Pacific Institute of Fisheries and Oceanography.

Normally, walrus populations—especially mothers and young pups—rest on giant chunks of sea ice floating in the Arctic Circle. They dive from the ice into the ocean shallows to hunt for clams and snails to eat, then rest on the ice for hours.

As global temperatures rise, sea ice in shallow waters where walruses usually feed melts. Here's the problem: Unlike seals—who are endurance swimmers—walruses can only swim short distances. The remaining sea ice is over deeper water and walruses can't dive down to the bottom and feed. That forces

Honeybee queens can quack.

the animals to retreat to the Arctic shoreline. The phenomenon is known as a "haulout."

Haulouts are a natural part of walrus life. Summer sends female walruses and pups onto shorelines every year. But in 2010, researchers from the U.S. Geological Survey (USGS) tracked a massive haulout on the Alaskan side of the Chukchi Sea. Ten to twenty thousand animals, mostly mothers and calves, were tightly packed along the shore. "It's something that we have never seen before in this area," said one researcher.

PANIC BUTTON

When a hungry polar bear, a hunter, or an low-flying airplane frightens walruses, they panic and head for the ocean. Tens of thousands of huge marine animals, some weighing as much as 3,700 pounds, stampede toward the sea. The calves can't keep up, so they're trampled by the adults. Bones are crushed; internal organs are punctured. Many do not survive.

"It's a real tragedy, and it's one we're going to see repeated more and more as the climate warms and the sea ice melts," said Rebecca Noblin of the Center for Biological Diversity.

What happens if sea ice continues to melt at the rate it's melting now? The USGS puts the chance of extinction (or serious population decline) among walrus at 40 percent by 2095. The Fish and Wildlife Service wants to protect the Pacific walrus under the Endangered Species Act. For now, they're on the waiting list.

THE POOP QUIZ

How much do you know about coprophagy?
If you're like most kids, the answer is, "What's that?"
Believe it or not, coprophagy is the act of eating poop.
If you're moved to learn more, take this quiz!

1. Which animal will lay its eggs in cow manure to be sure its babies will have plenty to eat?
a) Hummingbirds
b) Bearded dragons
c) Scarab beetles

2. What disease may be caused by eating chicken poop?
a) Food poisoning
b) Mad cow disease
c) Common cold

3. Where do they make cola from cow urine?
a) Coca-Cola bottling company
b) Mexico
c) India

4. Which dinosaur eats poop in Michael Crichton's book *Jurassic Park*?
a) *Procompsognathus*
b) *Triceratops*
c) *Tyrannosaurus rex*

5. Why do baby elephants eat their mother's poop?
a) It looks like chocolate
b) To get important digestive bacteria
c) To gross out their elephant big brothers

6. Which great apes sometimes eat their scat?
a) Gorillas
b) Chimpanzees
c) Both

7. Why do dogs eat cat poop?

a) It's easy to find.

b) It's especially high in protein.

c) It looks like candy.

8. What do termites make out of poop and saliva?

a) Smelly spitballs

b) Food for their babies

c) Towering termite nests

Answers on page 284.

*　　*　　*

PURPLE COW?

In 1895, Gelett Burgess penned this poem:

I never Saw a Purple Cow;
I never Hope to See One;
But I can Tell you, Anyhow,
I'd rather See than Be One.

Five years later, he wrote this:

Ah, yes! I wrote the
    "Purple Cow"—
I'm Sorry, now, I Wrote it!
But I can Tell you, Anyhow,
I'll Kill you if you Quote it!

ARREST THAT CUPCAKE!

Airport security takes a turn for the weird.

D ANGEROUS FROSTING
In December 2011, a Transportation Security
Administration (TSA) agent at the Las Vegas
airport seized Rebecca Hains's red velvet cupcake
before she could board her flight to Boston. The agent
claimed that the icing's "gel-like substance" posed a
security threat. The cupcake was packed in a glass jar,
and the agent thought the icing looked heavier than the
3-ounce carry-on limit for gels.

The TSA lets passengers take snacks, including
cupcakes with icing, in their carryon bags. But, to the
TSA agent, the cupcake seemed suspicious. A post on

the TSA blog said, "This wasn't your everyday, run-of-the-mill cupcake. Unlike a thin layer of icing that resides on top of most cupcakes, this cupcake had a thick layer of icing inside a jar."

Hains offered to eat the offending cupcake or put it into a zip-lock bag. The TSA agent iced both ideas.

STOP THAT PURSE!

Vanessa Gibbs never had a problem taking her purse on an airplane. Not until the Jacksonville, Florida, teenager tried to fly out of Norfolk, Virginia. "The [TSA] agent told me it's a federal offense to take anything shaped like a gun on board," Gibbs told a TV reporter after the incident. The purse wasn't shaped like a gun. But it did have a three-inch-long metallic gun *design* woven into it. The agent admitted the gun was a fake but still wouldn't let Gibbs take it on the plane. She had to check the purse like a piece of luggage or surrender it. Not only did Gibbs have to fly "purseless"—the delay made her miss her flight.

BAD HAIR DAY

Long hair could land you on TSA's "no-fly" list. Fifty-three-year-old Isis Brantley hasn't cut her tightly curly hair since she was 12. In September 2011, the TSA at Atlanta's Hartsfield-Jackson Airport stopped Brantley to search her hair for weapons.

"I heard these voices saying 'Hey, you! Hey, you, ma'am, stop! Stop! The lady with the hair!'" Brantley told a Dallas TV reporter. Then a female agent started "digging" into her scalp.

The TSA apologized to Brantley but defended the agent. "Additional screening may be required for clothing, headwear, or hair where prohibited items could be hidden."

OUCH!

On August 31, 2011, a man tried to sneak seven snakes and three tortoises through security at Miami International Airport. He stuffed them into nylon bags and hid them in his underwear. TSA agents discovered the critters as the man walked through a body scanner. He was arrested for "harboring reptiles in an unnatural habitat." The U.S. Fish and Wildlife Service got custody of the animals.

CHAIN REACTION

New York's Elmira-Corning Regional Airport TSA agents thought they'd seen it all...until a passenger tried to get through security with a fully-loaded power tool in his carry-on. The power tool was a chainsaw. But that wasn't the problem. The problem was the gas in the chainsaw's tank. Turns out you can take power tools on your travels as long as they're checked. After dumping the fuel and checking the chainsaw, the agents let the passenger through with enough time to make his flight.

*　　*　　*

FOUNDING FARTER

Your teachers probably told you that Benjamin Franklin was a great statesman, scientist, and inventor. They probably haven't told you that Franklin had more to say about farts than all of the other Founding Fathers put together.

"It is universally well known, that in digesting our common food, there is created or produced in the bowels of human creatures, a great quantity of wind.

Were it not for the odiously offensive Smell accompanying such Escapes, polite People would probably be under no more Restraint in discharging such Wind in Company, than they are in spitting, or in blowing their Noses."

—**Letter to the Royal Academy, 1781**

"He that is conscious of a Stink in his Breeches, is jealous of every Wrinkle in another's Nose."

—**Poor Richard's Almanac, 1751**

"He that dines on stale flesh, especially with the addition of onions, shall be able to afford a stink that no company can tolerate."

—**Letter to the Royal Academy, 1781**

"He that lives on hope, dies farting."

—**Poor Richard's Almanac, 1757**

NFL VS. AFL

Here's how the Super Bowl became…super!

BOING! BOING! SUPER BOWL

For football fans, the Super Bowl is the biggest sports event of the year. In 2011, fans paid, on average, $4,750 for a ticket to Super Bowl XLV (45). Those who couldn't go in person huddled in front of TV sets with chicken wings and chips, and cheered their lungs out for one team (or the other). But back in 1967, when the whole thing started, fans had no idea the annual championship would become a super-big deal.

For the first two years, the annual game was called the AFL-NFL World Championship Game. Everyone thought that was, well, pretty boring. Then, one day, Kansas City Chiefs owner Lamar Hunt watched his daughter play with a high-bouncing rubber ball called a Super Ball. Later, while talking about taking his team to the championship, Hunt said, "When we get to the Super Bowl…." The name stuck.

THE MOUSE THAT ROARED

The NFL had been around since 1920. Its teams were thought to be much stronger than those in the AFL,

which had been around for only seven years. Players, coaches, and fans of the NFL called the AFL "a Mickey Mouse league." The championship game was like pitting a mouse against a lion.

The first year, the NFL's Green Bay Packers won the championship easily, smashing the AFL's Kansas City Chiefs 35–10. The next year, the NFL won big again: Green Bay Packers 33, Oakland Raiders, 14. Most people expected the NFL's winning streak to continue in 1969. But one AFL quarterback disagreed: the New York Jets' Joe Namath. He was used to winning.

STARRING...BROADWAY JOE!

Namath had been a star quarterback at the University of Alabama. After college, he was drafted by the NFL's St. Louis Cardinals. But the NFL team had competition. The AFL's New York Jets wanted a star. They offered Namath $427,000—the highest salary any professional football player had ever received Namath took the offer.

In 1965, *Sports Illustrated* ran a photo of Namath wearing his green-and-white Jets uniform on its cover. Behind him is New York's famous Broadway theater district. A sign blazing with lights reads, "Football Goes Showbiz." *Sports Illustrated* called Namath a "real ring-a-ding-a-ding fingersnapper" and "a swingin' cat." (Hey, it was the '60s.) A fellow football player took one look at the cover and said, "There goes Broadway Joe." Despite the fancy new nickname, Namath still had to prove he could lead the Jets to a championship.

Before it sprays, the eastern spotted skunk does a handstand.

NFL REJECTS

Many of the Jets players had tried out for the NFL
earlier in their careers and not succeeded. Jets' receiver
Don Maynard had been released by the NFL's New York
Giants after catching a pitiful five passes in 12 games.
Defensive back Randy Beverly had been told he was too
small for the NFL. "These were players who had been let
go by or left out of the NFL," said Jets public relations
director Frank Ramos.

In the 1968 football season, Namath
led the Jets to the AFL championship,
with 11 wins and only 3 losses. He was
confident that his team would beat
the NFL's Baltimore Colts in the 1969
championship. At a banquet a few days
before the game, he said, "We're going to
win on Sunday. I guarantee it."

THOSE COCKY COLTS

The Colts were powerful. They had won 13 that season,
and lost only once. In the NFL championship game,
the Colts had beaten the Cleveland Browns 34–0. They
were considered one of the best NFL teams of all time.

Players and coaches from the NFL mocked Namath.
One Colts player told reporters that he expected his
team to win by 50 points. Vince Lombardi, the coach
of the Green Bay Packers, said that the Jets' chances of
winning were "infinitesimal" (too small to measure).

The Colts made several big gains early in the game.

They looked like the stronger team. But Namath kept encouraging his teammates. "He never let up all game," said Jets rookie John Dockery. "He'd pat everybody and keep telling us, 'C'mon, c'mon. Today is our day!'"

Things looked bad: the Colts recovered a fumble at the Jets 12-yard line. Then Randy Beverly made a diving interception in the end zone to get the ball back. After that, Namath completed several passes and fullback Matt Snell began to bash through the Colts' defense for big yardage. Soon the Jets had marched 80 yards. When Snell ran into the end zone for a four-yard touchdown, the AFL had its first lead ever in an AFL-NFL championship game.

JET-POWERED

The Jets' confidence grew, and for the rest of the game they played spectacularly, winning 16–7. It was one of the most surprising upsets in sports history. "Our biggest mistake was that we believed what we heard, that the NFL couldn't lose to an AFL team," said Colts tight end John Mackey.

The 1969 game was the first to officially be called the Super Bowl. And it lived up to that title, thanks to "Broadway Joe" Namath—chosen as the game's MVP (Most Valuable Player)—and the New York Jets who followed him into Super Bowl history.

YAY! I GOT IN!

These words are so new that they didn't even make it into dictionaries until after the year 2000.

Alpha geek (2012): the person in a group who knows the most about computing and related technology.

Bridezilla (2011): a woman who becomes obsessive or demanding while planning the details of her wedding.

Buttload (2011): a large number or amount.

Chillax (2010): calm down and relax.

Drama queen (2006): a person given to overly emotional performances or reactions.

Frankenfood (2009): a food that contains genetically modified ingredients.

Gazillionaire (2003): an extremely rich person.

Globesity (2011): an epidemic of obesity that has now spread worldwide.

LARPing (2012): Dressing in costumes and using props to become characters in Live-Action Role-Playing games.

Mouse potato (2006): a person who spends a lot of time using a computer.

Superbug (2010): a bacterium that is resistant to antibiotics.

Twitterati (2012): avid or frequent users of the social networking site Twitter.

As one of his first jobs, actor Brad Pitt wore a chicken suit to promote a Mexican restaurant.

DON'T FORGET TO VOTE!

Here's one way of getting out the rural vote.

R AISED IN A BARN
Several years ago, Brenda Gould of Newmarket, England, received a voter registration form from the local town council. It was addressed to the occupants of a building on her property. The problem? The building was a barn, so Gould ignored the form.

Then someone from the town council came by to ask why Gould hadn't returned the form. "We just thought they were being stupid," said Brenda. But her husband figured that if the town council really needed to know who was living in the barn, they'd tell them.

DOGGONE VOTERS!

Gould completed the form and registered its occupants: Henry and Sophie Bull, and Jake Woofles. No big deal, except...they're not people: Henry and Sophie are cows, and Jake is a dog.

It seems the town council has no sense of humor. The Goulds were fined $189 for giving false information on electoral forms and ordered to pay $208 in court costs. "It was a joke that's all gone a bit haywire, really," said Brenda. "I don't suppose we'll be doing it again."

Last part of the body to disintegrate after death: nails.

BRING ON THE GIRLS!

Think boy characters rule classic cartoons? Not so. These animated ladies can keep the boys in line and send the bad guys running.

GERTIE THE DINOSAUR—1914

One of the first animated films featured Gertie, a curvaceous lady dinosaur. Animator Windsor McKay created Gertie in 1911 as a stage companion for his vaudeville act. McKay would stand on stage in front of his audience and call for Gertie to join him. The film would roll, and Gertie, an animated "Brontosaurus" would appear to do tricks at his command. (Yes, they thought there was a dinosaur called the Brontosaurus back then.) Three years later, the film was shown in theaters. Gertie is considered one of the first cartoon characters with an appealing personality all her own.

MINNIE MOUSE—1928

Disney animator Ub Iwerks created Mickey Mouse for a short cartoon called "Steamboat Willie." But Mickey looked pretty lonely up there on the big screen. Iwerks was known for drawing animated sweethearts. So Minnie, the "flapper" mouse was born, complete with black stockings, short skirts, and oversized high heels that slipped off her tiny mouse feet. Minnie went on to be as important to Disney cartoons as her male counterpart.

BETTY BOOP—1930

During the Great Depression, Americans didn't have a lot to smile about. Jobs, food, and housing were hard to come by. So animator Max Fleischer created the adorable flapper with more heart than brains, Betty Boop, to cheer them up. Inspired by pop singer Helen Kane, Betty was a cartoon sex symbol, with pin curls, long lashes, and giant hoop earrings. She even showed up in a few Popeye cartoons and stole the show from the spinach-eating sailorman.

DAISY DUCK—1940

Disney decided Donald Duck needed a girlfriend, so the studio created the sophisticated Daisy Duck. In spite of Donald's cranky attitudes, Daisy falls hard for him in her first cartoon appearance. Daisy's no cartoon bimbo. Her calm, sensible approach keeps the hot-tempered Donald out of trouble, at least some of the time.

WONDER WOMAN—1941/1973

DC comics first introduced Wonder Woman to comic book fans in 1941. The red, white, and blue Princess of the Amazon flew an invisible airplane, wore deflective wrist bands, and whirled the Lasso of Truth to tame bad guys and protect all things noble. But she didn't come to life as an animated character until 1973. That's when she joined Batman, Robin, Superman, and Aquaman in the Super Friends series produced by Hanna-Barbera for ABC Television.

SHE-RA—1985

Filmation Studios introduced She-Ra as the twin sister and female counterpart to He-Man, the Master of the Universe. Unfortunately, She-Ra was raised by the Evil Horde and brainwashed by Shadow Weaver. He-Man tracks down his missing twin and breaks the spell she's been under. She-Ra then holds up her magic sword and says, "For the honor of Grayskull, I AM SHE-RA!" She might have added, "And I'm here to sell action figures!" Why? She-Ra and He-Man were among the first cartoon characters funded by a toy company (Mattel).

POWERPUFF GIRLS—1992

Animator Craig McCracken was a college student when he created the Powerpuff Girls. The Cartoon Network rolled out the series in 1998. Three tough little superstars were born. Blossom, Bubbles, and Buttercup were under the care of a brilliant scientist, Professor Utonium, in the fictional town of…Townsville, USA. The tiny tough girls helped the town mayor fight crime in 78 punch-happy episodes. The last one aired in March of 2005.

PRINCESS BUBBLEGUM—2010

Okay, she's a bubblegum girl infused with human DNA. But that didn't stop Princess Bubblegum from making cartoon history in the Cartoon Network's Adventure Time cartoons. For the first time, a female cartoon lead was more interested in science than in magic (or cartoon boys). Princess Bubblegum—a "millionaire nerd" who lives in the Land of Ooo—loves all branches of "geekdom," from rocket science to turtle farming. Animator Pendleton Ward created the show for Nickelodeon. Nick nixed it. The Cartoon Network didn't.

*　　*　　*

BRAND NEW LIFE-SAVING DEVICES

• **Air bag for your head.** It starts out as a collar worn around your neck. The collar contains a decompressed air bag. If you crash your bike...poof! The air bag deploys, and the protective air bag cushions your head.

• **E.M.I.L.Y the robot lifeguard.** The water's too rough for a rescue, or no trained lifeguard is around. What can you do? Throw E.M.I.L.Y. (an Emergency Integrated Lifesaving Lanyard) into the water! Steer the robot by remote control to the swimmer. The swimmer grabs on to E.M.I.L.Y. and waits safely for help to arrive.

UNIDENTIFIED SUNKEN OBJECT

*You never know what you might
find at the bottom of the sea.*

SUNKEN TREASURE

In 2011, a treasure-hunting company called Ocean Explorer did a sonar sweep of the bottom of the Baltic Sea between Sweden and Finland. What they were looking for: a shipwreck. What they found: a disk-shaped object 200 feet in diameter and as wide across as the wingspan of a jumbo jet. The object was sitting on the seafloor at a depth of 275 feet.

"We've heard lots of different explanations," said team leader Peter Lindberg. Some are pretty far-fetched. To *Star Wars* movie fans, the sonar image looks a lot like Han Solo's spaceship, the Millennium Falcon. To fans of Stonehenge, the object could be some weird undersea version of England's mysterious standing stones. Our favorite suggestion: the round disk might be a plug to an undiscovered world beneath the sea.

BACK TO REALITY

There are other, perhaps more real-world, ideas about the mystery object on the bottom of the Baltic Sea.

Some believe it could be the remains of a disk-shaped ironclad warship built in the 19th century by Russian naval architect Andrey Popov. Popov thought his round ships would make stable gun platforms that could operate in shallow water. He was wrong: His invention ended up on a list of "World's Worst Weapons." Did it also end up at the bottom of the Baltic? Lindberg says Popov's ships were much smaller than this disk.

Swedish submarine officer Anders Autellus thinks the object looks like a German submarine trap left over from WWII. The concrete structures were built to block British and Russian sub movements. Inside were large wire-mesh structures made to disrupt a submarine's radar signals.

Volker Brüchert, a professor of geology at Stockholm University, believes the sonar image shows something much more mundane: basaltic rock. This type of rock forms from hardened lava. Basaltic rock is "out of place on the seafloor," said Brüchert. "Possibly these rocks were transported there by glaciers."

CRASH LANDING

One other image showed up on sonar: a 985-foot flattened-out "runway" leading up to the object. Did the mysterious object skid along this path? In 2012, Lindberg's team spent 12 days in the dark depths exploring the object. They're still not sure what it is. "It's not *obviously* an alien spacecraft," Lindberg said. "It's not metal." Then again, he added, if an intelligent life form built a spaceship, "Why not make it out of stone?"

Longest boxing match on record: 110 rounds (Andy Bowen vs. Jack Burke, 1893).

SWEET ORIGINS

Love candy? Then you may be curious about how some popular candies got their start.

THE TREAT: Bubble gum
INVENTED BY: Walter E. Diemer, 1928
THE STORY: Diemer worked for the Fleer Chewing Gum company in Philadelphia in the 1920s. He wasn't a candymaker or a chemist. He was an accountant. But in his spare time—just for fun—he tested gum recipes in the company's lab. One recipe seemed to have promise—a tough stretchy goo. Diemer added pink food coloring to the mix. Not because he thought kids would love pink gum. Because pink was the only color on hand at the time.

Fleer named the chewy pink gum Double Bubble. Diemer taught the salesmen how to blow giant bubbles to help sell it. He loved to host bubble-gum-blowing contests for kids. When he died in 1998, his widow told *The New York Times* how her husband felt about inventing Double Bubble. "He would say to me: 'I've done something with my life. I've made kids happy.'"

THE TREAT: Life Savers
INVENTED BY: Clarence Crane, 1912
THE STORY: Ohio chocolate maker Clarence Crane had a problem. He needed a candy he could sell in summer—one that wouldn't melt in the heat. He

decided to make peppermint candies. Crane didn't want his candies to look like the pillow-shaped mints his competitors sold, so he punched holes in them. They looked like little life preservers, and he called them Life Savers. A year later, Crane sold the trademarked idea to Edward Noble for just under $3,000. Noble started the Life Saver candy company and wrapped the mints in the now-familiar foil rolls to keep them fresh.

THE TREAT: Marshmallows
INVENTED BY: Alex Doumak, 1948
THE STORY: Candy made from the marsh mallow plant has been around since ancient Egypt. The plant is a flowering shrub that grows in—you guessed it—marshes. The Egyptians ground up the plant's roots and mixed it with honey to make sweet candy. In the 1800s, French candymakers put the puff into marshmallow candies. They whipped sap from the marsh mallow root by hand. Then they put the fluffy candy into molds to harden. It was a slow process. Marshmallow manufacturer Alex Doumak wanted a faster way to make the puffy treat. He created a marshmallow "extrusion process." The marshmallow mix was piped through tubes. Then it was cut into equal pieces, cooled, and packaged. The new process allowed marshmallows to be mass produced.

TRICK OR TREAT, WHO WILL YOU MEET?

If you're curious about who you might marry, try one of these traditional rituals. Timing is everything. They only work on Halloween!

• Walk down a flight of stairs backward, carrying a mirror (and being very very careful). When you reach the thirteenth step, look into the mirror. You'll see a reflection of your future spouse.

• Have a big-time crush? Place an egg in front of a fire. If it sweats blood, you'll marry the one you desire.

• On Halloween night, peel an apple so that you have a long strip. Throw the peel over your left shoulder. It will curl into the shape of the first letter of your future spouse's name.

• Spread cornmeal on the floor by the side of your bed, then go to sleep. Ghosts will write the name of the person you'll marry in the cornmeal.

Are you a *librocubicularist*? You are if you read in bed.

- Walk around the outside of your house three times. After the third time around the house, you'll marry the first person you see. The catch? You have to fill your mouth with water and not swallow till you're done.

- In England, Halloween is also "Nutcrack Night." You and your sweetheart must throw nuts into a fire. If the nuts explode, run while you can! If they burn quietly, your future marriage will be a happy one.

- Hang up an apple and rub it with your spit. Stand six inches away, bend forward, and gently hit the apple with your chin. If it sticks, your true love will stick with you.

- Put on your pajamas and head into a cabbage patch at night. Pull up a cabbage. To find out what kind of personality your future mate will have, take a bite of the cabbage. It will be bitter or sweet.

- First, walk through a graveyard on Halloween night. Then put a cabbage above the door to your house. You'll marry the person it falls on when the door is opened. (If he or she forgives you for the headache.)

- Eat a salty food (like a herring), then walk backward to your bed and go to sleep without speaking to anyone. You may dream of your future spouse, who will bring you water to quench your thirst. If the water is in a gold or silver cup, you will be a rich couple. If it's in a glass, you'll be middle class. But if the water is in a tin cup— bad luck—you'll be poor. If no one appears in your dream and you have to get your own water, you'll never marry.

UNDERWEAR IN THE NEWS

These underwear actually deserve their 15 minutes of fame.

ELECTRONIC UNDERWEAR
Developed in 2003 at the
Philips Research facility in
Aachen, Germany
The Shorts Story: Electronic
underwear is designed for people
with heart problems. Sensors woven
into the undies monitor the wearer's
heartbeat. Then a microprocessor unit checks for signs
of dangerous heart rhythms. Dangerous rhythms include
ventricular tachycardia (too fast) or *bradycardia* (too slow).
If the underwear senses trouble? It sends a signal to a
Bluetooth-enabled mobile phone and calls for help.

The Downside: These undies put a new spin on the
term "tighty-whitey." Why? For the electrodes to work,
they have to be in contact with the skin. That means
the undies must fit tightly—especially in the groin area.

EDIBLE UNDERWEAR

Developed in 1998 by Russian scientists
The Shorts Story: Cosmonauts on the Russian space
station, Mir, had a problem. The space station didn't

have a clothes-washing machine, and they couldn't wash their underwear. Instead, they had to throw it away. Not good. "Cosmonauts identify waste as one of the most acute problems they encounter in space," said Vyacheslav Ilyin at the center for Biological and Medical Problems in Moscow.

Each cosmonaut was already creating about five and a half pounds of waste every day. To keep from adding underwear to that waste, they had to wear each pair for up to a week. (Ugh!) The solution: biodegradation. Ilyin's team of researchers developed bacteria that could eat and digest cosmonauts' cotton and paper underpants.

BALLISTIC BOXERS

Made by Cooneen Watt & Stone, the company that supplies the British armed forces

The Shorts Story: In 2011, the U.S. Marine Corps placed a $2 million order for underwear. The new undies were made to protect privates...privates. They look like the shorts worn by professional cyclists, and they're made from antimicrobial double-weave silk. The sturdy undies can't stop direct hits, but they can keep dirt and debris from entering wounds. And the antimicrobial agents in the silk prevent infection. Troops have already given their new shorts a nickname: "ballistic boxers." What's next? The military is considering outfitting personnel with metal cup protectors.

*　　*　　*

SKILL TOYS

The best thing about these ancient toys?
If you want to try them, they're still around.

DIABOLO

WHAT IT IS: A big butterfly-shaped spinning spool and two wooden "wands" attached at their tips by a long string.

THE SKILL: Also known as the Chinese yo-yo, the diabolo traces its origins back thousands of years to China. It was used by street entertainers at festivals, and to improve hand-eye coordination, flexibility, stamina, and strength. With enough practice, a person can toss the spool fifty feet in the air and catch it on the string before tossing it again. In the early 1900s, diabolos became a full-blown fad in the U.S. The fad was so big, cartoonists made fun of it. One cartoon showed a burglar caught red-handed. Why? He couldn't resist stopping to play with a diabolo he found in the house.

POI

WHAT IT IS: A soft hand-held ball, traditionally attached to a woven flax string, one for each hand.

THE SKILL: Poi involves rhythmically spinning and twirling weighted balls that hang from strings, ribbons, lengths of fabric. You can make simple poi by stuffing balls into two long socks. The fanciest models hy colors, blinking LED lights, or fluffy tassels at the ends of the strings. Some trained performers use poi that can be set on fire. (Consider yourself warned: Even these guys sometimes set their own hair on fire.) Poi are an invention of the Maori people, who are indigenous to New Zealand. Women used them to strengthen their hands for weaving. Men used them to build the wrist flexibility needed to battle with hand clubs and other weapons.

KENDAMA
WHAT IT IS: Two wooden cups centered on a spike (it looks something like a hammer). A ball with a hole drilled into it is connected to the spike by a string.
THE SKILL: The ball can be jerked or swung and caught in one of the cups. But one of the hardest tricks is impaling the ball on the spike. "After about twenty thousand failed attempts, you should be able to perform the trick flawlessly," says one instruction book. The kendama may have evolved from ancient toys that hunting cultures used to teach kids better hand-eye coordination. It's believed the toy came to Japan from Europe. France's King Henry II (1547–1559) was said to have played with an earlier version—called a *bilboquet*.

* * *

MR. SILLY PANTS

*Ever heard of Captain Underpants? It's a funny book series
about a superhero who parades around in—you guessed it—
his underwear. Here's how the silliness started.*

ARMPIT MUSICIAN

Dav Pilkey, the creator of Captain Underpants, was born in Cleveland, Ohio, on March 4, 1966. Even as a kid, he was a bit…different. For one thing, he laughed in his sleep. For another thing, while other kids were outside playing, he was inside drawing superheroes. And at school? Dav spent a lot of time sitting at a desk in the hallway or warming a chair in the principal's office.

Dav has something called Attention Deficit Hyperactivity Disorder. Most kids find it tough to sit still in a classroom for hours at a time. For kids with ADHD, it's nearly impossible. Some of them—like Dav Pilkey—do silly things when they get antsy. Dav held the class record for number of crayons stuck up his nose at one time. (No, we're not telling you how many.) He became an expert at playing songs with his armpits.

 And he stapled sheets of paper together to make "books" that he filled with funny stories and drawings.

READY FOR TROUBLE

"Every day before classes began, I would fill up my hallway desk with papers, pencils, and crayons," Pilkey said. "At some point in the day, I would do something really silly or disruptive and my teacher would snap her fingers, point to the door, and shout, 'MR. PILKEY—OUT!'"

One day, his teacher said the word "underpants" in class. Every kid in the classroom cracked up. "Underwear is not funny!" said the teacher.

She was wrong, and Dav new it. If just saying the word "underpants" could make kids laugh, what might happen if a superhero flew around the city in his underwear, giving wedgies to bad guys? That is how Captain Underpants was born.

THANKS, MOM & DAD!

Dav's teacher was not impressed. "You'd better straighten up, young man," she told him. "You can't spend the rest of your life making silly books."

Luckily, Dav's parents encouraged his artwork. They read his comics the minute they were finished. "They always laughed in all the right places and had good things to say about *most* of my stories," Dav said.

But…potty talk was not encouraged in the Pilkey household. So Captain Underpants mostly stayed in that hallway desk at school.

Once Pilkey went to college, things got better. His professors at Kent State University admired his creative

---

Exocannibals eat only enemies; *indocannibals* eat only their friends.

energy. They encouraged him to write and draw. At age 20, he entered a children's book writing contest and won! The prize? Publication of his first book: *World War Won*.

REVENGE OF CAPTAIN UNDERPANTS

Dav Pilkey still thinks about the teacher who banished him to the hallway. He wonders why creative energy isn't celebrated more in elementary schools. "I mean, if a kid can create a five-page comic book about Abraham Lincoln, why shouldn't that count?" he asks.

Perhaps success is the best revenge. More than 14 million books about Captain Underpants have now been sold. Dav is a popular guest at schools all over the country. He no longer gets sent to the hallway, but once in a while a teacher or principal or parent will say that his books inspire kids to make mischief. How does the successful author and illustrator respond?

"I usually just cup my left hand into my right armpit and pump my right arm up and down, creating a lovely flatulence noise," he says.

*   *   *

"When I was a kid making silly books out in the hall, I never dreamed that one day I'd be making silly books for a living. I used to get in trouble for being the class clown. Now it's my job."

——**Dav Pilkey, author and illustrator,**
Captain Underpants

RISE AND SHINE

Your parents have probably nagged you about breakfast being the most important meal of the day. But only Uncle John will share the weirdest, wackiest breakfast facts.

• The average person eats about 7,300 eggs in a lifetime.

• The morning menu at the Hilton hotel in Nairobi, Kenya, includes an ostrich egg omelet with strips of smoked impala meat.

• In Newfoundland, Canada, people use pancakes to predict the future. Each year on Pancake Day, bakers place tiny objects in the batter. The item you end up with is said to determine the course of your life. Bite down on a button and you'll become a tailor. An eraser? You'll be a teacher. And if you crunch into a coin, you'll be filthy rich. (Bite with care: If you choke on one of these items, your future could be shorter than hoped.)

• In early 2012, there were 289 people in Sydney, Australia, who set the Guinness World Record for "Biggest Breakfast in Bed." Dozens of bright pink beds were set up in a pedestrian mall. Up to eight people shared a single bed, and…breakfast was served.

• Too early for a fungus among us? Not in Mexico. An omelet filled with *huitlacoche*—black fungus-covered corn—is considered a breakfast treat there. The diseased corn is said to taste like mushrooms.

STOP AND SMELL THE PORTA-POTTY

There's nothing like the lovely fragrance of flowers. Except…
when they smell like dead animals. Or body odor.
Or a neglected litter box. Hold your nose, and read on!

OH, OOH THAT SMELL!
In 2012, researcher Greg Wahlert of the University of Utah discovered a new species of the *Amorphophallus* plant (also called the "corpse flower"). He found the plant on a tiny island called Nosy Ankarea off the coast of Madagascar. The plant is about four and a half feet tall. It's closely related to other plants that have been described as smelling like rotting meat, cheese, poop, fish, and urine. The new one has a long straight stem, and the flower sits at the top, looking a bit like a half-peeled banana.

How does the new plant smell? "Really foul and disgusting," said Wahlert. There are definitely hints of rotting animals in the flower's aroma, he added. "I would say carrion and feces."

Biology professor Lynn Bohs said the new species smells like "Rotting roadkill out in the sun, reeking. There's also a note of public restroom—a Porta-Potty smell." If you ever get a whiff of it, you might hope there's a real bathroom nearby. "Everybody I've talked to says they almost started puking when they smelled it," said Bohs. "It's horrid."

The Porta-Potty plant joins the distinguished list of the world's worst-smelling plants. Here are some others.

• **Lords and ladies.** Sounds like a sophisticated name for a flower, but these European plants smell like dog poop. The poopy smell attracts insects, which get coated in pollen before escaping. Then they carry the pollen to other flowers.

• **Stinking gourd.** The American desert plant *Cucurbita foetidissima* goes by many common names: buffalo gourd, coyote gourd, fetid wild pumpkin…but stinking gourd suits it well. The gourd is the size of a baseball and doesn't smell bad, but no one eats it. Why? Because the leaves smell like human body odor mixed with raw sewage.

• **Carrion flowers.** There are many varieties of carrion flowers, and some are very pretty. The African starfish flower looks like a reddish star, and the 10-foot-tall giant pelican flower of Brazil resembles a big red bird. But beauty isn't what attracts dung beetles and other bugs to the plants. It's the smell. Carrion flowers smell like rotting animal carcasses. Bugs come to the plants hoping to find a stinky rotten feast. They leave (disappointed, we're sure) with the plant's pollen stuck to their feet.

• **Indian almond plant.** Would you eat seeds that have a "putrid stench"? Believe it or not, some people eat them raw, fried, or even steamed. The stinky seeds taste like almonds. But eating too many can make you throw up.

• **Red-whisker clammyweed.** The plant lives in most of the western United States. Its name comes from its many long reddish-purple stamens called "whiskers." Just don't get too close. The smell is hard to describe, but it's said to be "weird and unpleasant."

• **Dragon lily.** This "dragon" is native to Greece and the Balkans. The plant's deep maroon lily-shaped "flower" isn't really a flower at all. It's a leaf. A long black pointy thing called a *spadix* sticks out of the leaf like a dragon's spiked tongue. For about a day, the whole thing smells like dungy rotten meat. The stench attracts a few flies that carry away the plant's pollen. And then…it stops stinking and just looks cool.

• **Java olive tree.** Guess what the Java olive tree smells like? Here's a hint: its Latin name is *Sterculia foetida*, which means "foul-smelling dung."

• **Duabanga grandiflora.** This grand tree can be found in the evergreen rain forests of Cambodia, Eastern India, Laos, Malaysia, Myanmar, Thailand, and Vietnam. But the tree's smell? If you have a cat, you can find the tree's smell closer to home: in the litter box. That is, if you've forgotten to clean it for a few days.

LITTER

Apache chief Geronimo was called Goyathlay by his tribe…

FUN WITH NUMBERS

If only math class could be this funny.

"There are three kinds of people: Those who can count and those who can't."

—**Anonymous**

"A pat on the back is only a few centimeters from a kick in the butt."

—**Dilbert**

"Mathematics—a wonderful science, but it hasn't yet come up with a way to divide one tricycle between three small boys."

—**Earl Wilson**

"Laughter is the shortest distance between two people."—**Victor Borge**

"To get something done, a committee should consist of no more than three persons, two of whom are absent."

——**Robert Copeland**

"Before you criticize someone, you should walk a mile in their shoes. That way, when you do criticize them, you're a mile away and you have their shoes."

—**Jack Handey**

"If A equals success, then the formula is A = X+Y+Z. X is work. Y is play. Z is 'Keep your mouth shut.'"

—**Albert Einstein**

NAME THAT BAND

*Hit rock bands have some pretty weird names…
and the stories behind them are just as weird.*

Maroon 5: The Grammy-winning band, which had its biggest hits in the early 2000s, was originally named Kara's Flowers. The four original band members were still in prep school at the time. "We were into Green Day, Weezer, and Beatles-inspired weirdness," said lead singer Adam Levine. The band split up when the four headed off for college, but two years later they were back together. They decided to call themselves Maroon. Because they'd added a fifth band member, they changed the name to Maroon 5. There are lots of rumors about the name, but its origin is still a closely held band secret. "We've only told one person," said Levine. "And his name's Billy Joel. He demanded I tell him, and I had to tell him." Rumor has it that the band changed its name in honor of a webcomic called "Pokey the Penguin." The comic featured a band called Yellow 5.

Vampire Weekend: These band members became friends in college and started making music and short films in 2006. Lead singer Ezra Koeneg was home from college one summer. He'd just seen the vampire flick *The Lost Boys* and decided to film an east coast version. The short film is about a boy named Walcott who travels to Cape Cod to warn the mayor that vampires are attacking the country. Ezra filmed the whole thing in only two days and called his movie *Vampire Weekend*. A few years later, he dug up the footage and decided the movie title would make a killer band name.

Chumbawamba: Best known for the 1997 hit song "Tubthumping," this alternative band started out with the name Skin Disease. (Ugh.) Official explanation for the name Chumbawamba: it's a nonsense word. Just a combination of syllables that rhyme (sort of). But band member Danbert Nobacon tells a different tale. He dreamed it up. In his dream, Nobacon needed to pee and went in search of a public toilet. He found two doors: one marked "Chumba" and the other marked "Wamba." Which one meant "Men" and which meant "Women"? Nobacon didn't have a clue, but if he put the two nonsense words together, it made a cool band name.

NASCAR drivers lose 5 to 10 pounds in a race. How? They sweat.

MEGASTORM

Could a giant rainstorm devastate California and turn its Central Valley into an inland sea? It's happened before, and scientists fear it could happen again.

WHO'LL STOP THE RAIN?

On Christmas Eve of 1861, rainstorms swept into California from the Pacific Ocean. Massive amounts of rain pounded California's Central Valley. And it didn't stop after a few days. It kept pounding and pounding, day after day, for 43 days.

Rivers running from the Sierra Nevada Mountains turned into raging brown torrents. Entire communities and mining outposts were swept away. By the end of the storm, the Central Valley had turned into an inland sea: 300 miles long and 20 miles wide.

Thousands of people died in the flooding. One-fourth of the state's 800,000 cattle were swept away. By the time it was over, ten feet of muddy, gunk-clogged water covered downtown Sacramento. The state's government had to flee to San Francisco and stay there…for six long months…until the area dried out.

SKY RIVERS

Studies of sediment deposits show that megafloods like this one happen in California about every 200 years. They're caused by "atmospheric rivers"—narrow bands of water vapor that hover about a mile above the ocean and extend for thousands of miles. Don't be surprised if you've never heard of rivers in the sky. Researchers didn't discover them until 1998. What they found: Outside of the tropics, 95 percent of all water vapor travels across the globe in long narrow moving bands. These bands carry moisture from the warm tropics to cooler, drier regions. Most of the time, they bring life-giving rain. But sometimes, they bring disaster.

ONE MISSISSIPPI…TEN MISSISSIPPIS

Imagine ten Mississippi Rivers floating side by side…in the sky. That's how much water atmospheric rivers can carry. When they hit inland mountain ranges like California's Sierra Nevadas, they dump monstrous amounts of water. Up to nine atmospheric rivers hit California every year. One of them even has a nickname: the Pineapple Express. (Yes. It comes from Hawaii.)

The U.S. owes the United Nations a billion dollars in unpaid dues.

In 2010, one massive atmospheric river dumped 26 inches of rain on parts of California, along with 17 feet of snow in the mountains. As temperatures rise with global climate change, scientists believe these rivers could grow even bigger. One scientist warns that global climate change may bring "megastorms of a scale that we may not have encountered, historically." In other words, future storms could make that 1861 inland sea look like a duck pond.

RAINY DAY PLANNING

More than 6 million people now live in the Central Valley, 1.2 million in Sacramento alone. Scientists say that if a megastorm like the one in 1861 happened today, more than a million people could be forced from their homes. Losses could total $400 billion. That's a bigger cost than what has been predicted for California's other "big one"—a mega earthquake.

The National Oceanic and Atmospheric Administration (NOAA) believes California needs an early warning system for megastorms. So NOAA is setting up four "atmospheric river observatories" along California's coast. Meteorologists will be able to train Doppler radar on the heart of approaching storms. If a storm shows signs of being a rain-dumping monster, people in the Central Valley may have a few days' warning. Of course a warning, or even an order to evacuate, might not be enough. Florida State University professor Jay Baker has studied the subject for decades. He says that in most cases, one-third to one-half of residents defy evacuation orders.

GROSS BODY QUIZ

Take this quiz to find out what you know about how much gross stuff your body makes.

1. How much do your feet sweat in a day?

a. 1 pint

b. 1 quart

c. 1 gallon

2. How much saliva does your mouth make in a day?

a. ½ cup

b. 2 cups

c. 5 cups

3. A full bladder of pee is about the size of what?

a. a tennis ball

b. a basketball

c. a softball

4. When you're healthy, how much mucus does your nose make in a week?

a. 1 cup

b. 3 quarts

c. 2 gallons

5. How many soda cans full of blood does your heart pump a minute?

a. 3

b. 5

c. 7

6. How many dead skin flakes does your body dispose of every day?

a. 36 million

b. 5 million

c. 10,000

Answers on page 284.

Baby wildebeests can run just minutes after they're born.

ROBO-PETS

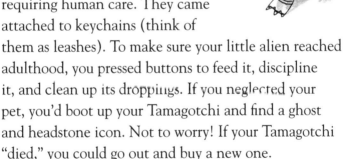

Parents won't let you get a real pet? No problem—these robots are just waiting to become a part of your life.

• One of the first truly popular digital pets was the Tamagotchi, from the Japanese company Bandai. The tiny egg-shaped pets launched in 1996 and hit the U.S. market in 1997. Tamagotchi pets were supposedly small alien eggs that hatched into creatures requiring human care. They came attached to keychains (think of them as leashes). To make sure your little alien reached adulthood, you pressed buttons to feed it, discipline it, and clean up its droppings. If you neglected your pet, you'd boot up your Tamagotchi and find a ghost and headstone icon. Not to worry! If your Tamagotchi "died," you could go out and buy a new one.

• Three years after the Tamagotchi's debut, Sony introduced the Aibo, a robotic dog for kids who couldn't have a real pet. Aibo couldn't fetch, but it could dance, recognize spoken commands, and respond to its owner's touch and actions. Unfortunately, with its sleek and hard plastic body, it didn't look much like a real dog,

---

Bugs Bunny's original name was Happy Rabbit.

and its $2,000 price tag made it a major splurge. Aibo was discontinued in 2006.

• PARO, by the Japanese company AIST, was released in 2003 as a caregiving robot to calm bed-bound patients. PARO is a white plush pet that looks like a baby harp seal. It coos, shrieks, and responds to human touch. It can even "learn." If you stroke PARO after a certain action, the robo-seal will repeat that action to be stroked again. If you hit it (not nice, kiddies), PARO remembers what it did before it got smacked and tries not to repeat that action. Hospitals, doctors, and nurses use the robot to comfort patients (those who aren't freaked out by robotic seals, that is). With a selling price of $6,000, the PARO is unlikely to ever make it out of a hospital ward.

• Looking for a pet with a bit more bite? Meet Kota the *Triceratops*, a robotic dinosaur from Playskool. At two feet tall and three feet long, Kota is big enough for preschoolers to ride. But don't get too excited—the *Triceratops* doesn't actually go anywhere. It does wiggle its horns and tail. And it roars…a lot. If you roar back, Kota will roar again…and again…and again. It will also swivel its giant head and blink its fist-sized eyes. When you get tired of all that roaring (and you will), scratch Kota four times under its chin to put the dinosaur to sleep. Awake or asleep, Kota sells for about $230.

*   *   *

There's a bridge in Lima, Peru, held together with egg whites.

THE RESTRICTED SECTION

There's something about banning a book that makes Uncle John want to read it more than ever. But, hey, you should decide for yourself.

The Book: *The Fighting Ground* by Avi
Banned When: 2008
Banned Where: Panama City, Florida
To Read or Not to Read: A parent found swear words in this book about the challenges a young boy faces during the Revolutionary War. But the executive director of the National Coalition Against Censorship says that parents have "no constitutional right to restrict all students' access to a library book because it conflicts with their personal views. Neither do they or their children have to read it."

The Book: *Bone* by Jeff Smith
Challenged In: 2010
Challenged Where: Rosemont, Minnesota
To Read or Not to Read: A parent wanted the Bone graphic novels pulled from the elementary school's library. The stories sometimes show characters smoking, drinking, and gambling. *Time* magazine called the series the "best all-ages graphic novel ever published."

The Book: *The Absolutely True Diary of a Part-time Indian* by Sherman Alexie
Banned When: 2010
Banned Where: Stockton, Missouri
To Read or Not to Read: The Stockton school district banned Alexie's book because of "violence, language, and some sexual content." A youth services librarian shot back in her blog that the book was "about a fourteen-year-old boy struggling with his decision to leave his family, his home, and his life behind because he wants a good education. This is the book that the county school board chose to remove? A book that celebrates a love of learning and the struggle that every person faces between making people happy and finding a life worth living?"

The Book: *And Tango Makes Three* by Justin Richardson and Peter Parnell
Banned When: 2008
Banned Where: Ankeny, Ohio
To Read or Not to Read: Some parents didn't want their children to read this true story of two male penguins raising a chick in the Central Park Zoo. Why not? They were concerned that it would promote homosexuality. The *Los Angeles Times* asked, "Why do gay penguins make people so mad? It's just [a book about] an orphan penguin with two daddies. Why can't people let it alone?"

*   *   *

MAGNETIC FACTS

If you're drawn to magnets, Earth's the place.

• What does it really mean when we say North Pole and South Pole? It means Earth is one giant magnet! Earth has a solid iron core surrounded by an ocean of hot liquid metal. Scientists think that's why our planet produces a magnetic field with two poles, north and south.

• A single magnet has one north pole and one south pole—just like Earth. These opposite poles attract each other. What's really weird: If you break a magnet in half, each half will have its own north and south pole.

• Every once in a while Earth's magnetic field flip-flops. What was north becomes south and vice versa. For most of the planet's history, flips came every million years. But since dinosaur times, pole reversal has been happening more often: about every 200,000 to 300,000 years. But don't worry. Polarity flips take hundreds to thousands of years to complete and don't put living things at risk.

• Some animals, such as pigeons, dolphins, and sea turtles, have the mineral magnetite in their bodies and brains. Scientists think this helps them navigate, acting like a built-in GPS (global positioning system). By sensing Earth's magnetic field, these animals can tell where they are and where they need to go.

• Magnetic fields have the power to ruin credit cards, cassette tapes, and floppy disks. Why? Each of those items has a long strip of magnetic particles that holds information. A magnetic field can scramble the data. (Which is why magnetic closures on wallets might not be such a good idea.)

• An MRI machine at a hospital is a big cylindrical magnet. The machine sends out radio waves that pick up signals from the body and turn them into a picture. MRI machines are thousands of times as strong as Earth's magnetic field. An MRI machine once sucked a policeman's gun right out of the holster, causing it to fire a bullet into the wall.

• Scientists at the University of Florida's Magnet Lab build and use magnets that have the most powerful fields on Earth. The lab holds 14 magnet-related world records and even has a magnet that weighs 35 tons—about as much as five adult blue whales.

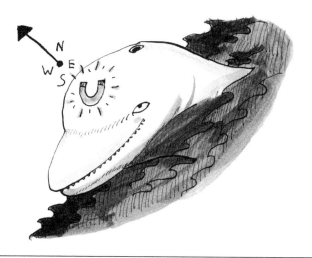

...than the band made selling albums.

THE SMELL OF MYSTERY

People keep swearing they see aliens and Bigfoot. But, proof?
These mysterious creatures don't seem to leave anything
behind but their smell.

ALIENS
Look like...The most
frequently spotted alien
is called a gray. It's a short,
slender, gray creature with two
legs, two long arms, a big bulbous
head, and large black almond-
shaped eyes.

Smell like...According to the Alien
Abduction Experience and Research Web
site, most witnesses claim the grays smell
like rotten eggs, ammonia, or sulphur. But some say the
aliens they encountered smell sweetly metallic.

Few people ever get the chance to smell space. But
International Space Station Officer Don Petit has done
just that. "The best I can come up with is metallic,"
Petit said. "A rather pleasant sweet metallic sensation."
Former NASA astronaut Thomas Jones is a veteran of
three spacewalks. Jones remembers a smell like burnt
gunpowder or the ozone smell of electrical equipment.

That smell shows up on a shuttle or in a space station after a spacewalk. It can only be smelled on suits and equipment that have been used in the vacuum of space.

BIGFOOT

Looks like... Most people who say they have seen Bigfoot describe a tall creature that looks something like a cross between a human and a large ape. The creature is totally covered with hair, usually reddish-brown to auburn. It stands between 6 and 12 feet tall. And it is almost always spotted alone.

Smells like... Bigfoot smells musky and outdoorsy, most witnesses say, like all wild animals. The smell is not unusually strong or unpleasant. But 10 percent of witnesses tell another story: Bigfoot is a big stinker.

Dr. W.H. Fahrenbach of BigfootEncounters.com reports that some witnesses say Bigfoot's smell is "unbearable and overpowering, like being wrapped in dirty diapers."

Before her death, primatologist (ape specialist) Dian Fossey described the "fear scent" of a mountain gorilla. If the gorilla fears for its life, the smell can be "overpowering" and "gagging," Fossey said. Why? According to Fossey, giant apes release "diarrheic stool" (poop) as they run. That strong poopy stench can be smelled as far as 80 feet away.

Is it possible Bigfoot is an unknown primate with fear reflexes like those described by Fossey? Without proof, it's impossible to say.

Fast food: about 20 percent of all meals in the U.S. are eaten in a car.

FOUR HUMORS

Uncle John would have had a tough time living thousands of years ago. Why? Because folks back then had very different ideas about "humor."

DON'T MAKE ME CRANKY

Doctors of antiquity (not just old-timey, but more like old-old-OLD-timey) believed that a person's health and personality were determined by four fluids—blood, yellow bile, phlegm, and black bile. (Yes, it's just as disgusting as it sounds.) These fluids were called *humors*. Each one was believed to be produced by an organ in the body.

Those old-old-OLD-timey doctors thought that each fluid had a connection to one of Earth's four "natural elements": air, fire, water, and earth. The humors could influence not only a person's health, but a person's mental health and appearance, too. Let's say your body produces too much of one humor fluid: You might have yellow skin. Too little of another: You might be cranky.

Ancient physicians also believed that balance was the key to good health and happiness. So they tried to understand and control the four humors.

THAT'S BLOODY AWFUL!

Today, when we think of blood pulsing through the body, we picture the heart pumping fresh blood to our organs and bringing it back for recycling. But ancient

Cats have 32 muscles in each ear.

doctors thought blood came from another organ: the liver. That's right, they thought the liver was the center of the circulatory system. (Boy were *they* wrong!)

"The liver is the source of the veins," wrote Roman anatomist Galen, "and the principal instrument of sanguification." *Sanguification* is how the body makes blood. So Galen—and other ancient docs—believed the liver didn't just pump the blood through our veins, he thought the liver *created* blood.

Blood was seen as hot and moist. Its element: air. Because blood is red, ancient doctors thought a healthy person would have a rosie complexion. They thought a blood-rich person would be lively and energetic. On the downside, a "sanguine" person might be impulsive and hot-tempered.

If the body was overheated or feverish, doctors figured the culprit was too much blood. If left untreated, they believed, too much blood would lead to serious problems like seizures or maniacal behavior (you might go nuts). Too little blood, on the other hand, might lead to a lack of energy.

The cure? Bloodletting. The practice started with the ancient civilizations of Egypt and Greece. And it continued for thousands of years, all the way until modern times. Bloodletters (doctors) used a small knife to open a vein in the arm, leg, or neck. Then they drained the "excess" blood into a bowl. It was the ancient equivalent of "take two aspirins and call me in the morning."

YELLOW MAKES A BITTER FELLOW

Yellow bile, or "choler," was believed to be an acidic fluid that helped with digestion. Ancient doctors believed yellow bile was stored in the gall bladder. (And, guess what? They got that one right!) This little organ was viewed not only as the source of choler, but also as a storage bin for "bitterness of spirit": sour moods. (Now we know bile is made in the liver, but stored in the gall bladder.)

Doctors believed that the gall bladder was attached to both the brain and the heart. (Not…it sits just below the liver.) And they believed the organ had a big influence on a person's emotional state. A healthy gall bladder would restrict the flow of yellow bile, keeping its owner happy. Too much yellow bile might cause negative emotions, like feeling bitter.

Yellow bile's element is fire: hot, dry and violent. Doctors belived people with high levels of yellow bile in their systems would have fiery personalities. A choleric person might be cruel and unkind, or terribly unlucky and given to fits of envy. Ancient doctors expected people with too much yellow bile to be thin and sickly, with yellow or jaundiced skin and sharp features. And their dreams might be filled with fire, lightning, fighting, and…yellow things.

The best thing to balance yellow bile: something bitter. Bitter herbs, bitter medicines, bitter foods… all were thought to have "an almost magical ability to regenerate and restore" a yellow bile imbalance.

DOWNRIGHT SNOTTY

Phlegm (sounds like "flim") represents all "colorless secretions" of the body. Translation: sweat, saliva, tears and snot. These fluids were believed to be "lubricants and coolants" for the body. Phlegm's element: water.

Doctors believed that these lubricating and cooling substances came from the lungs and the brain. They even thought the lungs and brain were made of phlegm. (Yo, snot brain!) For phlegm to do its job, it needed just the right amount of moisture. Too much moisture in the brain might lead to epilepsy, an illness that causes seizures. Too much phlegm in other parts of the body might lead to tuberculosis. (By the way, turns out epilesy is actually a disease of the brain, and TB is primarily a lung disease.)

Phlegmatic persons were pasty, pale, and tended to suffer from obesity. An overabundance of phlegm made a person lazy. Phlegm-imbalanced people might seem dull and lifeless. As if all the spark had gone out of them.

To get rid of all that nasty phlegm, ancient doctors often prescribed...peppers! Cayenne, Black Pepper, and Long Pepper (Pippali). After all, hot is the opposite of cold. Spicy ginger could also be helpful. As for cold foods and drinks? If you had too much phlegm, you had to avoid them: cucumbers and melons; cold drinks and juices; milk and dairy products were off the menu. So was sugar and sweets. (Sorry, kids!)

THE ORIGINAL BLACK HUMOR

The final humor, black bile, was considered the most toxic substance produced by the body. Black bile was like pollution. It was cold and dark and dry, like soft dirt. So its corresponding element was earth. Doctors believed black bile could seep into other bodily fluids. Once it did, the body parts would darken to create a deeper color in the skin or the blood. Black bile was thought to cause dark moods. If the imbalance went unchecked, madness might set it.

The only thing that kept black bile from destroying the body was the spleen. The spleen was believed to contain this dangerous bile. "The spleen [is] the receptacle of melancholy as the gall bladder of gall," wrote English physician William Harvey in 1653, "wherefore the spleen causes one to laugh." (Actually, the spleen doesn't contain bile at all. It contains white blood cells that fight germs and infections.)

The cure: laughter! Laughter was believed to be the sign of a healthy spleen. To battle black bile and the onset of madness, doctors recommended "jesting, singing, music, pictures and dancing." Oddly—or maybe not so odd—there are modern doctors who still swear that laughter makes the best medicine of all.

ANIMATED QUOTES

Cartoon characters speak their minds.

"I shall call him Squishy. And he shall be mine. And he shall be my Squishy."

—Dory (to a jellyfish which then stings her), *Finding Nemo*

Pumbaa: "'Hakuna Matata' is our motto."
Simba: "What's a motto?"
Timon: "Nothing. What's a motto with you?"

—*The Lion King*

Agnes: "My caterpillar never turned into a butterfly."
Edith: "That's a Cheeto."
Agnes: "Oh."

—*Despicable Me*

"You're in kindergarten, right? I used to love kindergarten. Best three years of my life."

—Mike, *Monsters, Inc.*

Mom: "Is that broccoli?"
Milo: "No, that's vomit, but I understand the confusion."

—*Mars Needs Moms*

"I was thinking, you know, we have a surplus of dragon-fighting Vikings, but do we have enough bread-making Vikings or small-home-repair Vikings?"

—Hiccup, *How To Train Your Dragon*

BUGS BY THE MOUTHFUL

When you spot a creepy-crawly on your wall, is your first instinct to grab it and chow down? After you read this, it might be!

TASTY TERMITES

In Ghana, many people live in rural areas. They spend the spring months planting seeds for summer crops. There isn't a lot to eat during planting season. But there are plenty of termites. Monsoon-type rains during springtime drive the winged termites from their red mud mounds. Ghanaians grab the critters and roast them, fry them, or grind them into flour.

THE SIX-LEGGED GOURMET

In Japan, picky patrons at fancy restaurants dine on insect larvae. In the larval stage, insects don't have the crunchy hard-to-digest body parts that fully grown insects develop. Favorite dishes include boiled wasp larvae, the fried pupae of silk moths, and aquatic fly larvae with soy sauce and sugar.

FREE SAMPLES

Not many Americans are gung-ho about eating bugs. David George Gordon—known as the Bug Chef—is on

---

A 100-gram serving of crickets has as many calories as a Big Mac (560).

a mission to change that. Gordon is the author of *The Eat-a-Bug Cookbook*. He travels to food festivals around the country and hands out free samples. He serves up his signature dish—Orthopteran Orzo—in a paper cup. What is it? Orzo pasta sprinkled with…crickets. He's also been known to give out white-chocolate-and-waxworm cookies and tarantula tempura samples.

BITE-SIZED TREATS

If you're not too grossed out to try eating bugs, here are some guidelines. Myke Hawke, who trains Green Beret soldiers for wilderness survival, cautions against eating bugs that are furry, brightly colored, smell bad, have spikes or barbs, or bite. Once you have your bugs, remove any sharp or pointy parts like stingers, shells, legs, wings, and pincers. If you're in the mood for worms, soak them for a day, then roast, boil, or bake.

Still feeling squeamish about eating bugs? You might want to know: They're probably already in your diet. That's because a few insects in the food supply don't bug the U.S. Food and Drug Administration (FDA).

• The FDA doesn't mind if a 300-gram jar of apple butter has up to 15 whole insects in it.

• A 400-gram bag of frozen broccoli can contain up to 240 aphids or mites.

• There can be up to 400 insect fragments in a 50-gram container of ground cinnamon. (Bet you didn't even taste them!)

KILLER TOYS

*Think all toys are fun and games? Then you
probably haven't played with these!*

THE TOY: AQUA DOTS (Moose Enterprises)
THE FUN: These tiny, round, plastic beads
used to create art projects were named the 2007
"Toy of the Year" in Australia.

THE TERROR: A 10-year-old kid ate about 80 of
the tiny dots (don't ask) and…stopped breathing.
Turns out, the colorful beads were made in China, and
a chemical called *1,4 butanediol* was an ingredient in
their shiny coating. When swallowed, the butanediol
converted to *gamma hydroxyl butyrate* or GHB. That's a
dangerous toxin. If swallowed in high doses, it can cause
slowed heart rates, drowsiness, unconsciousness, seizure,
coma, and even death. Parents and toy stores freaked
out, and the toymaker had to recall 4.2 million of the
play sets.

THE TOY: WII REMOTES (Nintendo)
THE FUN: When Nintendo launched its Wii video-
game console in November of 2006, it was considered
revolutionary. The Wii handheld remotes and the
movements of the people holding them would literally
guide the action within the games. Play Wii tennis, and
the controller became your racket. Clench the remote

in your hand, and it became the boxing glove. What could go wrong?

THE TERROR: People were so focused on the game, they forgot to notice the people and things around them. Pretty soon, people in Wii households were sporting black eyes, fat lips, and stitches. And when a sweaty hand lost its grip mid-swing, the Wii remote could break its wrist safety strap and fly right through windows...and flat screen TVs.

Nintendo responded by putting stiffer warnings in the system and in the packaging for the remotes. In December of 2006, they replaced the flimsy straps with sturdier versions less likely to break in the heat of a game. But accidents still happen. Even Nintendo—one of the top-selling console creators in the world—can't "fix" human error.

THE TOY: SKY DANCERS (Galoob)
THE FUN: Who wouldn't want a beautiful 9-inch-tall fairy doll with "magical wings and pretty dresses"— especially if that doll would launch like a twirling helicopter-Barbie with the yank of a string? The toys flew off shelves after their 1994 debut. And *The New York Times* predicted they would be "all the rage."
THE TERROR: They were...for a few years. As it turned out, foam wings might have been a good safety precaution. Sky Dancers didn't float gracefully from girl to girl as shown in commercials. They slammed into faces and other body parts, causing cuts, bruises,

missing teeth, eye damage, and a broken rib. After 150 confirmed injuries, nearly 9 million of the toys were recalled in June of 2000.

THE TOY: POKÉMON COLLECTOR BALLS (Equity Marketing, Inc)
THE FUN: In 1999, when Nintendo's creative team released a feature-length Pokémon film, Burger King decided to give the toys away as kids' meals prizes. They offered 57 different plastic Pokémon characters, each in its own three-inch Pokéball. Kids flocked to the fast-food restaurant to "catch 'em all."
THE TERROR: The promotion was a hit, until a few Pokéballs ended up in the hands of toddlers. Thirteen-month-old Kira Alexis Murphy's older sisters had gotten the toys from Burger King. Somehow, half of a Pokéball ended up in the toddler's playpen while her mom was in the shower. Kira picked it up and put it over her nose and mouth. When she inhaled, the container formed an airtight seal. By the time her mother found her, the toddler had suffocated. A few months later, an 18-month-old girl's lips turned blue before her father could pull the ball off her face. Then a four-month-old baby was suffocated by a Pokéball. Burger King recalled 25 million of the toys, but that wasn't enough for Kira's mother. Burger King had described the toys as being for "all ages," rather than for patrons ages 3 and up. She sued the fast-food chain, the toymaker, and the safety-testing company.

THE TOY: WACKY CLACKER (Win Industries)

THE FUN: Picture two small hard plastic balls dangling from equal lengths of tough, flexible string. Now picture a small plastic handle at the center of the equal lengths of string. You've just imagined the popular 1960s toy called "Wacky Clackers." Set the balls in motion, and you can make a noise that's hard to duplicate. (Wooden versions had been used to frighten birds away from crops in the 19th century.)

THE TERROR: Hold the clacking balls too close to body parts, and you get bruises, chipped teeth, and black eyes. If the balls shatter, the danger increases: from knocks and bruises to stitches and possible blinding. In 1971, the Consumer Protection Agency issued warnings. There had been thirteen injuries, including three deaths, one a strangulation when the clacker cord wrapped around a girl's neck. The other two deaths involved infants who swallowed the clacker balls and suffocated. Even so, the hard plastic clackers weren't banned until the late 1980s. Today's version has foam balls, which seems to miss the whole point (but is probably safer).

PRINT ME A...

When Gutenberg invented the printing press in 1439, print was totally 2D. My, how times have changed!

THE THIRD DIMENSION

Regular printers lay down ink in layers. 3D printers work the same way. But instead of ink, they lay down materials such as polymers, resins, metal, glass, nylon...even chocolate. It's easier than you might think. First, the 3D printer slices up the object's computerized design into hundreds of printable layers. Then it lays down two-dimensional layers, layer upon layer, and fuses them together with a laser. What can a 3D printer print?

A...Burger

In the "Star Trek" television series and movies, a "replicator" was used aboard the Starship Enterprise to create meals. Totally sci-fi? Not anymore: Using electronic blueprints called FabApps, 3D printers can now build everything from chocolates to cheese puffs, layer-by-layer, using edible ink. In 2011, Cornell Creative Machines Lab printed out a hamburger patty, complete with layers of ketchup and mustard.

A...Drone

In July 2011 the world's first "printed plane" took off from a soggy grass landing strip in Britain. The craft was an uncrewed drone, like those commonly used in everything from crop dusting to military surveillance. The plane's creation took only one week from drawing board to 3D flyable craft. "It's very hard to believe this aircraft was just a pile of dust last Friday," said one of the project's lead designers.

A...Jawbone

In June of 2011, an 83-year-old woman in Belgium received the world's first 3D printed jawbone to replace one damaged by infection. The jaw is made from titanium (a metal), not human bone. "We use metal powder for printing," said medical engineer Ruben Wauthle. "To print organic tissue and bone, you would need organic material as your 'ink.' Technically it could be possible—but there is still a long way to go before we're there." Other body parts that may be printed for medical use in humans in the future: cartilage, blood vessels, and skin.

A...House

Robotics expert Enrico Dini is the inventor of the world's largest 3D printer: the D-Shape "robotic building system." His goal? To print 3D houses on Earth and 3D igloos on the moon. Dini's printer uses nothing but ordinary sand (or moon dust) and a binding agent. The D-Shape printer has the potential to create a two-story dome, complete with stairs, walls, and spaces for plumbing (don't forget the bathroom).

HAUNTED HISTORY

If you'd like extra chills for your next cultural outing,
Uncle John recommends these cold-spots.

THE HUNTER MUSEUM OF AMERICAN ART (Chattanooga, Tennessee)

The oldest building of the Hunter Museum was built where a home once stood. Nothing creepy about that...until you add that fact that an elderly woman was murdered in that house in the early 1900s. Some say the woman, Augusta Hoffman, roams the museum's halls at night. Why? She seems to like art. Employees say they see her carefully examining paintings before she fades away, showing a flash of her bashed-in head.

STONEWALL JACKSON MUSEUM (Winchester, Virginia)

Thomas Jonathan "Stonewall" Jackson, a general for the Confederate Army during the Civil War, might have been amused to hear that his namesake museum is not only haunted, it's *hyperhaunted*. The museum was built on top of a haunted battlefield over a haunted cave. Inside the haunted museum lights go on and off. Artifacts—such as a nineteenth-century black dress—move around. When a visitor snapped a photo, it seemed to reveal a skeleton sitting next to the dress.

THE TOWER OF LONDON (London, England)

The Tower has earned a reputation for being one of the most haunted places in Europe. And no wonder—hundreds of murders, executions, and disappearances have taken place there. High-profile ghosts such as Guy Fawkes (the guy who tried to kill King James I in 1605) and Ann Boleyn (the Queen beheaded by Henry VIII in 1536 to make way for wife number three), are regularly seen in the Tower. Visitors have even been attacked. "Several women who slept there have reported waking in the middle of the night feeling they were being strangled," said Major General Geoffrey Field, who governed the tower until 2006.

CASTLE OF GOOD HOPE (Cape Town, South Africa)

Travel writer Stacey Vee says that the Castle of Good Hope is "packed to the rafters with ghosts." One is a giant, ferocious black dog that lunges at visitors and then dissolves in mid-leap. The creepy castle also features a painting of peacocks. The painting—so we're told—is cursed. Legend has it that you're doomed to a nasty death if you move the artwork. Then there's the *Donker Gat* (dark hole)—a windowless dungeon that often flooded during high tide. A dozen helpless prisoners may have drowned there.

HAPPY COSMONAUTICS DAY

Each year in April, Russians gather for an out-of-this world celebration of the first man to rocket into space.

STOP THE BUS!

On April 12, 1961, the bus carrying 27-year-old Soviet cosmonaut Yuri Gagarin made an unscheduled stop on its way to a launch pad at Baikonur Cosmodrome in Kazakhstan. The young cosmonaut was about to be strapped into the spherical top of the *Vostok 1* rocket and—if all went well—make history. But first, he needed to hop off the bus and "take a leak."

Once at the launch pad, Gargarin boarded the capsule and settled into his seat. Then he started joking with rocket designer Sergei Korolyov about not having enough food for the "long" adventure he was about to take? "You've got sausage, candy, and jam to go with the tea," Korolyov said. "Sixty-three pieces—you'll get fat!"

TEST DUMMIES

Just a few weeks before, two other adventurers had blazed the trail in a prototype of Gagarin's craft. One was a life-size dummy nicknamed Ivan Ivanovich, and

---

The tallest snowman ever built was taller than a 12-story building.

the other was a dog named Zvezdochka ("Little Star"). Ivan and Zvezdochka completed one low-Earth orbit that lasted 115 minutes.

Ivan ejected upon re-entry and landed near the Ural Mountains. The guys back at mission control had decided to write the word "Model" across Ivan's forehead in case anyone thought he was a real man. Zvezdochka made it safely back to Earth, too. And that cleared the way for Gagarin's mission: to be the first human to blast into space and orbit Earth.

WE'RE OFF!

Just below Gagarin's spherical capsule was a string of fat round oxygen/nitrogen tanks that would supply him with air to breathe outside of Earth's atmosphere. Below that were enormous fuel tanks that would power the rocket's leap from Earth's gravitational pull and propel the 10,417-pound rocket into space.

At 9:00 a.m., the rocket blasted from the launch pad. "Poyekhali!" Yuri shouted. ("We're off!") For the next 108 minutes, the new Soviet hero orbited the globe. Mission scientists had been worried that weightlessness might cause him to black out. But the cosmonaut kept talking. "The sensation of weightlessness feels nice," he told ground control. "Everything is swimming."

SO CLOSE, AND YET...

Back in the U.S., astronaut Alan Shepard got a phone call. He'd been preparing for NASA's first manned space flight. Now he was hearing from mission control that Gagarin had snatched the space-race victory out of his hands. The frustrated astronaut saw a silver lining in Gagarin's success: The cosmonaut had proven that a man could withstand the stresses of launch and landing. Just 25 days later, Shephard blasted into space aboard the *Freedom 7*.

DAYS OF GLORY

U.S. President John F. Kennedy congratulated the Soviet Union on their "outstanding technical achievement." Leaders around the world echoed that message. A year later, Nikita Khrushchev, leader of the Supreme Soviet, proclaimed Gagarin's launch date a national holiday. He called it one of Russia's "Days of Military Glory." Russians have celebrated Cosmonautics Day ever since.

In 2011, on the *Vostok 1* flight's 50th anniversary, the United Nations General Assembly took the holiday worldwide. April 12 became the International Day of Manned Space Flight. To mark the anniversary, Russian officials released 700 pages of top-secret reports documenting the historic flight to readers all over the world. (That's how we know about the sausages.)

As for Gagarin's "pit stop" on the way to his historic launch? It started a tradition. Since that first flight, all male crew members on the way to the Baikonur launch pad leave the bus. They stand at the left back wheel and—*ahem*—relieve themselves.

TOO MANY NAMES!

Some parents will do anything to embarrass their kids.

PACKING A PUNCH

Boxing fan Brian Brown of England decided to name his daughter after the 25 men who had been world heavyweight champions. So, in 1974, Maria Sullivan Corbett Fitzsimmons Jeffries Hart Burns Johnson Willard Dempsey Tunney Schmelling Sharkey

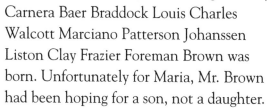

Carnera Baer Braddock Louis Charles Walcott Marciano Patterson Johanssen Liston Clay Frazier Foreman Brown was born. Unfortunately for Maria, Mr. Brown had been hoping for a son, not a daughter.

Maria had a baby girl of her own in 2007. Her name? Autumn…plus those same 25 middle names.

GIRLY FROM A TO Z

Back in 1883, Arthur Pepper gave his daughter a name for every letter of the alphabet. That's right: He named her Anna Bertha Cecilia Diana Emily Fanny Gertrude Hypatia Inez Jane Kate Louise Maud Nora Ophelia Prudence Quince Rebecca Sarah Teresa Ulysis Venus Winifred Xenophon Yetty Zeno Pepper.

GO-GO GADGETS!

Think technology is all about computers? Think again.
The latest tech can help you see better, stay warm,
and could even save your life.

The Gadget: Color-blindness Glasses
What It Does: People who are color-blind can't see all the colors most people see. That's where these "smart" glasses come in. There are two types of lenses. One corrects for a color blindness called *deuteranomaly*. What does deuteranomaly do? It makes it tough to tell the difference between red, green, yellow, brown, and pink. The other type of lens corrects for *protanomaly*. These lenses help the wearer tell the difference between shades of green, red, brown, and purple.
Cost: $600–$800

The Gadget: Self-heating Gloves
What It Does: These handwarmers store energy from a battery. Sensors in the gloves detect if the fingers get too hot or too cold. The gloves' fingers are lined with a paper-thin film. When the fingers get cold, the film becomes denser and power flows through it more easily. When the fingers warm up, the film conducts less power.
Cost: $200–$390

The Gadget: Emergency Mobile Phone
What It Does: In the fall of 2012, Hurricane Sandy devastated New York City and the New Jersey shore. Millions of people were without power for weeks. Here's the thing: Without power to recharge your cell phone, you can't make calls—even if you really, really need help. This emergency phone works on a single AA battery. If unused, it can last for up to 15 years. And when you do need it, that AA battery gives you 10 hours of service.
Cost: $90 and up

The Gadget: Wi-Fi Smart Pen
What It Does: Take notes (or doodle) in class and the pen's Wi-Fi sends your notes to an internet "cloud." The pen can also record your teacher's words of wisdom (or your friend's lame jokes). You can retrieve your notes and audio recordings on any smartphone or tablet.
Cost: $170 and up

The Gadget: Washable Keyboard
What It Does: Makes it okay to eat PB&J sandwiches or mustardy hot dogs while keyboarding. This computer keyboard has drainage holes so you can hand-wash all the goo off the keys. And the key characters are UV coated so the letters won't fade. Each key will last up to five million keystrokes…even with a whole lot of snackin' goin' on.
Cost: $40

JUST DESSERTS

We're usually too busy chowing down on dessert to worry about its history, but as the locavores say, it's good to know where your food comes from.

Brownies: The first brownies may have been one of the tastiest mistakes ever made. Legend says that around 1900, a housewife in Bangor, Maine, was trying to bake a chocolate cake. She wanted the cake to rise with a nice dome on top, but she messed up, and the cake collapsed. Company was on the way, though, so she had to do something. In a panic, she cut the cake into squares and served it that way. *Voilà*—the brownie was born.

Sundaes: Ice-cream sundaes also came into being around the turn of the 19th century (a rich time for desserts, it seems). In 1881, a vacationer at Ed Berners's soda fountain in Two Rivers, Wisconsin, asked Ed to give him some ice cream with chocolate sauce on top. Ed refused. The thought was crazy—chocolate sauce was only for making sodas. "You don't want to ruin the flavor of the ice cream," he said. But the vacationer insisted, Ed caved, and the sundae became a sensation.

Eton Mess: Eton mess is an English dessert that consists of broken-up meringue pieces, sliced strawberries, and whipped cream mixed together. Its origin is debated, but one story says that the dessert came about when a meringue and a berry dish were jumbled together during a bumpy car ride. Another says that an lively Labrador retriever created the dessert in the 1920s during a cricket match at Eton College. The Lab sat on a pavlova (another meringue treat) and smashed it to bits.

Doughnuts: Dogs aren't the only animals inventing desserts. According to Dutch immigrants, the first doughnuts were made when a cow kicked a pot of boiling oil over onto some pastry dough. Those doughnuts didn't have holes, though. The holes were the brainchild of Hanson Gregory, an American sailor who lived in the late 1800s. Hanson was annoyed that the dough in the middle of pastries didn't cook through. So he did something about it. "I took the cover off the ship's tin pepper box, and I cut into the middle of that doughnut the first hole ever seen by mortal eyes!" he said.

ASK DR. FART

*Here's how the world's leading expert on
fart science got his start.*

SILENT BUT STINKY

Have you ever heard someone say that silent farts smell worse than loud ones? That's a common belief. But, according to Dr. Michael Levitt, it's not always true. The smell of a fart comes mostly from a gas called *hydrogen sulfide*, and there can be just as much of it in a loud fart as in a quiet one. Dr. Levitt should know—he's the world's foremost authority on farting. (Of course, there aren't many others in the field.)

"Farts have been good to me," Levitt says. But he also says his career could have only happened in the U.S. "In other countries, no way would a scientist study farts. But for reasons I can't completely figure out, farting is considered wrong in America, and people are worried about it."

THE SCHOOL OF FARTS

Believe it or not, the study of farting has a proper name: *Flatology.* Flatulence is the scientific word for having intestinal gas. So why did Dr. Levitt choose this field in the first place? When he was fresh out of medical school, he worked for a well-known doctor named Franz Ingelfinger. Dr. Ingelfinger suggested that Dr. Levitt study intestinal gas. The field wasn't crowded, so there was an opportunity to get his fart studies noticed. "I would have a good chance of being successful," Levitt said, "since no one else was studying it." Dr. Levitt was right. And it all started with one case.

FART LOG

In 1976, a 28-year-old man came to see Dr. Levitt. He had a rather embarrassing problem. For about five years, he'd been farting—a lot. How much? Luckily, the young man had been keeping a log to record his farts for two years. Weird…but as it turns out, good. Levitt found seven other people who would be willing to keep a log of every fart they made for a week. At the end of the week, he compared the averages. Volunteers: 13.6 farts per day. His patient: 34.

Worse still, the average person shoots out between 500 and 2,000 milliliters of gas per day. But when Dr. Levitt measured *this* patient's farts, he discovered that the young man was releasing an average of 5,520 milliliters per day—more than two to ten times the average. What could possibly be causing so much gas?

GOT MILK?

Levitt knew that foods could be to blame. One likely culprit: complex carbohydrates. The simple carbohydrates in foods are easy to digest, Levitt says. Others—such as pastries, potatoes, citrus fruits, apples, and breads—are much tougher to digest. And some complex carbohydrates—beans, carrots, raisins, bananas, onions, milk, and milk products—can't be broken down by normal metabolism. When these get into the digestive tract, the results can be...explosive.

Dr. Levitt altered his patient's diet to try to find the mystery food causing all those farts. First, he had the young man eat only non-fart-causing foods for three weeks: meat, fish, grapes, berries, potato chips, nuts, and eggs. The young man's fart log showed his fart-per-day rate go from 34 to 17, not far above average.

Then Dr. Levitt added a quart of milk per day to his patient's diet. *Boom!* Within 24 hours, the young man had logged in 90 farts. Mystery solved: the patient was lactose intolerant. He lacked the enzyme that digests milk. From then on, the young man avoided dairy products (and hopefully stopped keeping a fart log).

*　　*　　*

THE TOOT TRAPPER

In 1998, Dr. Levitt and other researchers at the Minneapolis Veterans Medical Center tested a product called the Toot Trapper. It was invented by a man who farted so often that his co-workers demanded that he be moved into a separate room with a door. The device was a thin fabric-coated foam cushion coated with activated charcoal. It was to be worn inside the pants, supposedly to absorb fart odor and cut down on embarrassment. What did Dr. Fart decide? It works!

BACON DERBY

It's a four-legged squeal to the finish line.

Four pigs ran a race at the county fair. Each was dressed in a colorful vest. The race ended in a snout-to-snout finish. In fact, the pigs finished so close together that officials had a hard time sorting out which pig had won. They also couldn't deterimine the order of the other three pigs. Think you can figure it out? Here are the facts our indecisive officials agreed on:

1. Pinky finished behind Tulip.

2. Rosie finished ahead of Jade.

3. The pig in the yellow vest won the race.

4. Tulip wore purple.

5. Pinky did not finish last.

6. The pig dressed in blue finished ahead of the pig dressed in green.

Bonus: Which color did each pig wear?

Answer (and how to find it) on page 285.

POLIO DIDN'T STOP...

For centuries, this terrifying disease struck down millions, rich and poor, famous and unknown. Here's a look at a few polio victims who not only survived, but thrived.

...Eleanor Abbott (1910-1988) from inventing a wildy popular board game. Abbott was a retired teacher when she ended up in a hospital recuperating from polio. She was bored. And she knew the patients in the hospital's children's ward were desperate for something fun to do. So Abbott created...the Candy Land board game.

...Frank Mars (1883–1934) from becoming the founder of the M&M Mars chocolate company. Frank caught polio shortly after he was born. He spent his whole life in a wheelchair. But during his childhood years at home, his mom taught him to make seriously yummy candy. He started inventing his own recipes, and that eventually lead to Milky Way bars, Snickers, 3 Musketeers, and, of course, M&M's.

10 percent of U.S. electricity comes from energy taken from...

...**Franklin Delano Roosevelt** (1882–1945) from becoming president of the United States. Roosevelt was a 39-year-old politician when he contracted polio. It put him in a wheelchair for life. After he became president in 1933, Roosevelt celebrated his January birthday with Birthday Balls to raise money for the care of polio patients. "Once you've spent two years trying to wiggle one toe, everything is in proportion," Roosevelt said.

...**Alan Alda** (b. 1936) from becoming an actor. Best known for his role as Hawkeye Pierce in the TV series M*A*S*H, Alda got the disease at age 7. At the time, treatment involved wrapping burning-hot woollen blankets around the legs. Then the muscles had to be firmly massaged to stretch them and keep them from going lame. It hurt...a lot. Alda said it's like "your parents are torturing you against their own will." He had to endure that pain "every two hours, for months."

...**Francis Ford Coppola** (b. 1939) from directing movies such as *The Godfather* and *Bram Stoker's Dracula*. Coppola contracted polio at age 8 and spent almost a year in bed, unable to move his legs. "I became interested in the concept of remote control," he said. "I think because I had polio, I'm good with gadgets, and I became a tinkerer."

...**Jack Nicklaus** (b. 1940) from golfing. Nicklaus was already an excellent golfer at age 13. He was playing an exhibition game when he started feeling stiff and his joints started to ache. Doctors thought he had the flu, but it was polio. Nicklaus recovered, but he battled

...dismantled nuclear weapons, including Russian nuclear bombs.

sore joints throughout his career. That didn't stop him, either. Nicklaus was named "Golfer of the Millenium" by every major golf publication in the world.

...**Itzhak Perlman** (b. 1945) from becoming a world-famous violinist. "One afternoon I was standing up on my bed in Tel Aviv, and I felt a little weak. And I had to sit down. I was four years old. I was wild riding bikes and stuff like that.... And all of a sudden, I felt like I couldn't do it, and that was it," he recalled. The disease caused permanent paralysis in his legs. But he quickly learned to use braces and crutches to walk. And then, he learned to play the violin. He's played on TV's *Sesame Street*, at the White House, and with the New York Philharmonic to perform at The Concert to End Polio.

*   *   *

EVERY LAST CHILD

In 1955, Jonas Salk's polio vaccine became widely available. Doctors quickly began to vaccinate as many kids as possible, all over the world. By 1994, the Americas were certified as "polio free." In 2004, 80 million children across 22 countries in Africa received immunizations. Outbreaks still happen. In 2011, there were 650 polio cases reported around the world. There was even an outbreak in China, a country that had been "polio free" since 1999. The World Health Organization plans to fight the disease until "every last child" has been vaccinated.

FFLLBBLLLTTT!

Some thoughts on farting.

"You don't have to be smart to laugh at farts, but you'd be stupid not to."

—Louis C.K.

"I don't wanna talk to you no more, you empty headed animal food trough wiper! I fart in your general direction! You mother was a hamster, and your father smelt of elderberries!"

—*Monty Python and the Holy Grail*

"I hate how my new Converse shoes make fart sounds when I walk. People have been giving me funny looks all day."

—Chelsea Chanel Dudley

"Few things make me sadder than when someone farts on a plane and I can't escape it."

—Olivia Munn

"I did not win the Nobel Fart Prize."

—Bart Simpson

"A woman who can fart is not dead."

—the Comtesse de Vercellis

"Us giants is making whizzpoppers all the time! Whizzpopping is a sign of happiness. It is music in our ears! You surely is not telling me that a little whizzpopping is forbidden among human beans?"

—Roald Dahl, *The BFG*

ASTRONAUT GROOMING TIPS

Good grooming on Earth takes time. Good grooming in space takes gravity-defying creativity.

TIP 1: WEAR A DIAPER

As astronauts prepare for lift-off, they lay strapped into acceleration couches, feet toward the sky, head toward Earth...for up to three hours. The

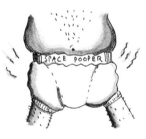

urge to pee can be irresistible, so they wear something NASA calls a "Maximum Absorbency Garment." Is a MAG just an adult diaper? Pretty much. The MAG also has a nickname: "Space Pooper."

TIP 2: STORE AND RECYCLE

Once in space, astronauts have to do their business without water for cleanup and...without gravity. That makes it much harder to make sure what comes out, goes down. The solution to this problem is a $19 million strap-in toilet. The modern space toilet comes equipped with two high-tech suction tubes: one for Number 1 and one for Number 2. Feces are stored in special tanks for disposal back on Earth. Urine goes into a recycler to be cleansed and converted to...drinking water.

TIP 3: DON'T FORGET TO STRAP IN

Why are there straps on astronaut toilets? Because space farts can be powerful things. Release a big one, and it can act as a thruster. If the straps aren't engaged, the space traveler can launch right off the toilet.

TIP 4: BRING A SQUIRT GUN

Earth showers are easy because gravity keeps water pumping through the shower head. In the zero gravity of space, water is harder to handle. Astronauts use a special air-powered squirt gun to force water onto wash cloths. Then they use the wet cloths for a speedy wash-up.

TIP 6: HOLD THE HAIRCUT

On short missions, astronauts don't need to shave or cut their hair. On longer trips, they shave and trim their hair almost the same way they do on Earth. But without gravity, there's a problem: all those little hairs can fly off and float around their living space. The solution? Use a vacuum tube to suck up the little hairs as you shave or trim and keep those quarters hair-free.

TIP 7: BRUSH, BRUSH, SPIT

Any toothpaste will do in space, but without water and sinks, where's an astronaut supposed to spit? The well-groomed astronaut squeezes a little toothpaste onto a toothbrush to clean the teeth but instead of spitting into a sink, spits into a tissue. A space traveler can also use edible toothpaste and just swallow (*Yum!*).

The crunch of a potato chip comes from exploding air pockets.

PLANET BACTERIA

Humans may seem like the most important species on Earth. But guess what? They weren't the first.

BEAT BY BILLIONS
Bacteria were the first life-form on Earth. These microscopic single-celled creatures colonized the planet 2.7 to 2.9 billion years ago. But the first modern humans—*homo sapiens*—have only been around for 200,000 years or so. When we did show up, bacteria immediately colonized *us*. Here are some amazing facts about the tiny creatures who call Earth (and our bodies) "home."

- Bacteria are so important to human health, we couldn't live without them. They help digest our food and produce vitamins. "Good" bacteria keep "bad" bacteria from making us sick.

- There are far more bacteria on Earth than humans. How many? Five million trillion trillion! The numeral is so big we can't write it out here. (If you want to see what it looks like, write a five with thirty zeroes after it.) Humans haven't yet reached the ten billion mark.

- Bacteria live everywhere on Earth: in deserts, oceans, hot springs, the polar ice caps…even in the sky.

- Bacteria reproduce by splitting in half. Some can split once every 12 to 20 minutes. That means a single bacterium can produce billions of offspring in one day.

- Bacteria come in many different shapes, but the four main shapes are spherical (ball-shaped), short rods, threads, and spirals.

- Most bacteria can't be seen without a microscope. The largest known bacteria—*Thiomargarite namibiensis*—is the size of the period at the end of this sentence.

- Only one percent of known bacterial species can make humans sick.

- Babies are born without bacteria, but from the minute they leave their moms' wombs bacteria invade their bodies. As babies take their first gulps of air or sips of milk, bacteria enter their mouths, ears, noses, stomachs, and then move beyond to inhabit the entire body.

- Each of us carries around about two pounds of bacteria…just in our guts.

- Bacteria found in yogurt can help fight tooth decay.

- In 2010, oil-eating bacteria bloomed around the Deepwater Horizon oil leak in the Gulf of Mexico. The helpful bacteria may have eaten as much as sixteen percent of the oil that spilled into the ocean.

- Bacteria found in poop can hitch a ride on water droplets when the toilet is flushed and land on anything nearby…your toothbrush, for example.

PHRASE ORIGINS

Match each saying with its origin.

1. Pass the bar

a) In 16th century England, a wooden bar separated lawyers and judges from the riffraff in the courtroom.

b) Lawyers must be sober to defend their clients. So "passing the bar" meant going past all the bars between the lawyer's home and the courthouse...without stopping in for a drink.

c) In a relay race, a runner must hand off the baton to a team member. In the law, someone who is already a lawyer must hand an iron bar to someone who wishes to become a lawyer. The bar represents the iron fist of justice.

2. A real dud

a) When a bomb hits the ground but doesn't go off, it makes a muffled earthy noise that sounds like "dud." A dud came to mean anything that doesn't do what's expected.

b) Dudley Do-Right was a dimwitted character in a 1960s cartoon. Since that time, anyone thought to be less than brainy has been "a real dud."

c) A "dud" is an article of clothing. Cast off clothes were used to dress scarecrows. Scarecrows were called "dudmen"—as in not *real* men. In time, anything fake or less than cool became a "dud."

3. Caught red-handed

a) Picking blackberries turns hands red, but so does swiping them from the kitchen. Being caught red-handed first referred to children caught with evidence of berry-stealing on their hands.

b) In the bloody 15th century, a murderer found with blood still on his hands was literally caught "red-handed."

c) During medieval times, thieves were "branded" by having their hands dyed red. If something went missing, people with red hands were questioned first.

4. Turn a blind eye

a) During a sea battle, British commander Lord Nelson was signaled to withdraw from combat. Nelson, who was blind in one eye, put his blind eye to the spyglass. He said he saw no such signal flag and gave the order to fire.

b) Justice is said to be blind. So turning a blind eye came to mean believing that if your cause was just, you did not have to follow the rule of law.

c) Pirate captains don't wear eye patches because they've lost an eye. They wear them so they can "turn a blind eye" as crewmembers plunder ships. That way, they can swear in a court of law that they're not guilty of piracy.

Pound for pound, ground beef costs more than a new car.

5. Smoke and mirrors

a) CIA agents always fog up mirrors in rooms with their breath. That way, if the mirror is actually a two-way mirror, no one in the next room can spy on the spy.

b) The saying started with magicians who used real smoke and mirrors to fool audiences.

c) When fighting fires, the only way to tell where the actual fire is behind all the smoke is to hold up a mirror. Flames can be seen on the mirror's surface.

6. Close, but no cigar

a) Instead of stuffed toys, games of skill at fairs once gave out cigars. So if you threw the ring and missed at Ring Toss, the guy manning the booth would say, "Close, but no cigar."

b) The phrase was first used in playing horseshoes. Gentlemen often had cigars clenched in their teeth while tossing horseshoes. So the cigar became a unit of measurement to award—or not award—a point.

c) Originally, the phrase was "As close to perfection as a Cuban cigar." Now that smoking is known to cause lung cancer, the term that used to mean "almost perfect" has come to mean "a near miss."

Answers on page 285.

*　　*　　*

"Be nice to nerds. You may end up working for them."

—**Charles J. Sykes**

GAMERSPEAK

If you don't want to look like a noob next time you play, you might want to study these insider video-gaming terms.

Noob: A new player, or a gamer who plays badly.

Pwn: Originally a typo for "password owned," it now means you've been beaten (owned).

Bunny hopper: A gamer who jumps around a lot.

Gratz: Short for congratulations.

Gib: Think "giblets." This one means blowing people up.

Hax: Hacked code that allows a gamer to cheat on a game to gain unfair advantage.

Woot: Hooray! or Wow!

Boss: The main bad guy in any game.

Mob: A group of hostile enemies in a live online game.

Train: A group of mobs chasing after another single mob.

Mule: A secondary character used to store the items you need.

Twitch games: Games that require lightning-fast reflexes.

Zerg: Overwhelming force—using sheer numbers instead of skill.

Buffs: Online magic spells that strengthen a character.

Squishy: A character with no armor or defenses.

WHO WANTS TO BE A BILLIONAIRE?

We thought you'd like to know the secret to getting rich. Here it is: work. As for the first jobs of some of the world's richest people? You might be surprised.

Rich guy: Warren Buffet, Investment Wiz
Net worth: $47 billion
First job: Newspaper delivery boy

Buffet started his empire with $1,200 he'd saved from two newspaper routes. He invested the money in real estate, buying 40 acres of Nebraska farmland that he leased to a farmer. He was 14 years old when he made that first investment. Now, he's the third-richest person on the planet. Not bad for a paperboy.

Rich guy: Oprah Winfrey, Media Mogul
Net worth: $2.7 billion
First job: Grocery store clerk

Winfrey faced not only poverty but abuse as a kid. She tried to run away at age 13 and almost ended up in a juvenile detention home. All the beds were filled, so Winfrey was sent to live with her father. He had strict rules, including a curfew, and a requirement that she read a book and write a book report every week. Pretty soon, Winfrey was an honor student, winning prizes for public speaking and drama. She kept working until she had her own talk show—it aired in 140 countries around the world—her own magazine, and a TV station. Winfrey was the first African-American woman to become a billionaire.

Rich guy: Michael Bloomberg, New York City Mayor
Net worth: $18 billion
First job: Parking lot attendant

Bloomberg credits scout camp in the "wilds of New Hampshire" with teaching him to be self-sufficient and to work well with others. Taking ice-cold showers, drinking "bug juice" (grape punch), peeling potatoes, and doing dishes are all part of what he remembers as the "highlights" of his summers. But instead of grousing about the tough life at camp, he used the work ethic he learned there to make him a stronger person.

Rich guy: J.K. Rowling, Author Extraordinaire
Net worth: $1 billion
First job: Researcher for Amnesty International

The world's richest author got teased as a kid: "rolling stone" and "rolling pins" were among the names neighborhood kids thought were funny plays on her last name. Rowling loved to tell tales and would force her younger sister Di to listen. "I was much bigger and could hold her down," Rowling admits. Even if she never tells

---

Total cost of NASA getting a man on the moon: $40 billion.

another story, she'll probably rake in big bucks from the Harry Potter brand for the rest of her life. Right now, she makes money from Harry Potter books, films, merchandise, and the Wizarding World amusement park in Orlando, Florida.

Rich guy: Guy LaLiberté,
Cirque du Soleil Founder
Net worth: $2.5 billion
First job: Blew fire and walked on stilts

Laliberté grew up in the small town of St-Bruno, Quebec, Canada. After high school, he decided to hitchhike across Europe. He spent his first night in London on a public bench with his backpack, two accordions, a mouth organ, spoons, and less than $1,000 in his pocket. During his travels, he learned the art of fire-breathing and stilt-walking, and became a street performer, working for small change to pay for the basics. When he returned home, he had enough experience to land a contract to stage a street show for Quebec's 450th anniversary celebration. Now, Cirque du Soleil's shows bring in a million dollars a night.

Rich guy: David Geffen, Music Mogul
Net worth: $4.6 billion
First job: Usher at CBS Studios

Geffen grew up poor in a tough Brooklyn neighborhood. He was a small kid who got beat up often by bullies. Living in a one-bedroom apartment with his family, he had to sleep on the family's couch. He did poorly in high school and flunked out of college, but his gift for spotting musical talent made him a millionaire by the time he was 26. Geffen discovered groups like Crosby, Stills and Nash; the Eagles; and Nirvana, and turned singers like Joni Mitchell and Bob Dylan into stars. He also co-founded Dreamworks, which produced animated hits such as *Shrek*, *Chicken Run*, and *Kung Fu Panda*.

Rich guy: Li Ka-shing, Business Superstar
Net worth: $26 billion
First job: Selling watchbands

In 1939, Li was a 11-year-old Chinese kid whose father was a primary school principal. That year, the Japanese invaded China. Schools were shut down, and Li's family fled to Hong Kong. Three years later, his father died of tuberculosis. Li had to drop out of school and take a job at a watch-strap company to support his family. Despite 16-hour workdays, he kept studying, buying second-hand textbooks from teachers. By age 21, Li had started his own company making plastic flowers to sell in the U.S. Today, Li is the eleventh richest person in the world. His nickname in Hong Kong: Superman.

BIZARRE BAROMETERS

When is a barometer not a barometer? When it's a sore knee, a headache, or a swallow trying to catch a meal.

Hark how the chairs and tables crack!
Old Betty's joints are on the rack;
Her corns with shooting-pains torment her
And to her bed untimely sent her…
'Twill surely rain—I see with sorrow
Our jaunt must be put off to-morrow.

**—from Prognostications from the Weather,
Robert Merry's Museum, November 1844**

I KNEED MORE SUNSHINE

In the 1800s, there was no Doppler radar or TV meteorologists to warn people of weather changes. They looked for signs in nature and collected rhymes like the one about Betty's joints to predict the weather. Instead of poo-pooing such folk wisdom, researchers at Tufts University in Massachusetts decided to test whether someone's knees really could predict a weather change.

In 2007, they selected 200 patients who had arthritis in their knees for a study. The patients lived all across the United States, so their knees were responding—or not—to different weather, depending on where they lived. The patients tracked the pain level in their knees and then went online every two weeks to share the information. Researchers then checked their pain levels against local weather reports. The results? Patients *did* feel more pain when a storm was approaching. In fact, they acted like human barometers.

Barometers measure changing atmospheric pressure, or the weight of air. Storms are linked to low pressure and blue skies to high pressure. When storms are about 12 to 24 hours away, the weight of the air presses down on a barometer—or a sore knee.

"Instead of super-duper Doppler 8000, they should just get a room full of people with arthritis and ask 'Is it going to snow tomorrow or not?'" says Dr. Stephen Makk, a spokesperson for the American Academy of Orthopedic Surgeons.

OH, MY ACHING HEAD

Changes in weather can also affect people who get migraines. A migraine isn't an ordinary headache. It's an intense throbbing pain in one area of the head. The pain is so bad it often brings on nausea and vomiting. A migraine can last for hours or even days. Sufferers are very sensitive to light and sound. All someone with a migraine wants to do is curl up in a dark, quiet place and wait for the pain to go away.

Hospitals report that more migraine sufferers show up in emergency rooms after a drop in barometric pressure than when the barometer is rising. Scientists have studied the connection between barometric pressure and headaches since the 1970s. They haven't come up with proof that weather changes are to blame. But many migraine sufferers say the proof is in their pain.

HARD TO SWALLOW

Humans aren't the only animals that seem to act like barometers. The traditional weather rhyme, "Swallows high, staying dry; swallows low, wet will blow," might seem silly until you look at the facts. When the barometric pressure is high, heat rises up from the ground and creates thermals. Thermals lift the swallows' prey—insects—high into the air. So swallows have to fly high to swallow them up. The low pressure that signals wet weather forces insects back toward the ground. And where the bugs go, the swallows follow.

More Animal Weather Forecasters

- Ladybugs tend to swarm when the temperature reaches 55 degrees Fahrenheit. That's earned them this proverb: "When ladybugs swarm, expect a day that's warm."

- In Germany, tree frogs may help kids gauge the temperature without going outside. In the wild, tree frogs climb up tree branches when the weather gets warmer. When the weather cools, they climb back down. It's said that a tree frog kept in a glass jar with a little wooden ladder will go up and down the ladder as the weather warms and cools.

- Keepers at Virginia's Metro Richmond Zoo swear that tigers love rain and snow. But what about rougher weather? If a thunderstorm is brewing the tigers get edgy and start to pace. "And then without fail, the thunder starts, and lightning," said zoo director Jim Andelin.

- Dogs have a few weather tricks, too. According to his owner, Rachel Henkle, a yellow lab named "Polar" can predict snow. He warns the family by barking and running around. Henkle claims he's 100% accurate. If the forecast is for a 30% chance of snow, but Polar barks and runs around, it snows. If the forecast is for a 90% chance of snow, but Polar doesn't bark? No snow.

- Even out on the range, cows prefer hanging out together than wandering off alone. But if you see a herd huddling together like a football team, that probably means the cows have sensed an oncoming storm. Cows huddle up in storms for warmth and security.

If the Statute of Liberty were a real person, her sandals would be size 879.

AMAZING COMEBACKS

Next time your team is hopelessly trailing toward the end of a game, don't give up. These guys sure didn't.

BUZZER BEATER

It was the final seconds of the East Regional final in the 1992 NCAA basketball tournament. North Carolina's Duke University had scraped its way into overtime. But Kentucky had squeezed ahead, 103–102 and seemed to have wrapped up the victory. Duke would have to go the length of the court to score, and only 2.1 seconds remained on the clock.

Duke forward Grant Hill took the ball out of bounds. His teammate Christian Laettner stood at the other end of the court, waiting by the free-throw line for a long, unlikely pass. The 6-foot-11 Laettner waved his lanky arms to give Hill a big target. Hill made a perfect 75-foot pass. Laettner caught it with his back to the hoop, dribbled once, spun around, and took a 15-foot shot. The ball fell through the net, and Duke had an impossible win.

"Everything was in slow motion, like one of those scenes from *Hoosiers* or *The Natural*," said Hill, referring to two classic sports movies with incredible endings. But this slow-mo ending was real.

THE SHOT HEARD ROUND THE WORLD

With six weeks to go in the 1951 baseball season, the American League's New York Giants were in last place. Then—incredibly—they won 16 games in a row. And they kept on winning until they caught up with the Brooklyn Dodgers. The two teams ended the season tied, both with records of 96–58. A three-game playoff was set to decide which team would play in the World Series. After splitting the first two games, it all came down to one. And the decisive game was played in the Polo Grounds, the Giants' home field.

With two outs in the bottom of the ninth, the Dodgers led, 4–2. The Giants had runners on second and third, when star outfielder Bobby Thomson came to bat. Pitching for the Dodgers: Ralph Branca, who had yielded a game-winning homer to Thomson in the first playoff game just two days earlier.

Branca threw a strike. His second pitch was a high inside fastball. Thomson leaned back and smacked the ball into the left-field bleachers for a home run, winning the game and the National League pennant. It was the first game ever to be televised nationally, and Thomson's game winner became known as "The shot heard round the world."

...used 1,460 eggs every day during shooting.

FOOD OR NOT FOOD

Which of these items don't belong on a list of snacks?
Bananas, cookies, rubber, glass, dry wall. If you picked the
last three things, you haven't met these food freaks.

JUST EAT IT

Frenchman Michel Lotito holds the Guinness World Record for "Strangest Diet." Lotito (who died of natural causes in 2007) could eat metal, glass, rubber, and other inedible materials without getting sick. Huh? It seems his stomach lining was *twice* as thick as a normal person's. "I consider myself half animal, half man," said Lotito. "I love animals. I feel a bond with them. When I don't eat glass or iron, my jaw aches like a young dog's that craves to chew a bone." Guinness gave him a brass plaque, which he promptly ate.

SHARP CRIMINALS

In the late 1990s, Ronald and Mary Evano discovered that they could get rich by swindling insurance companies. The plan? Eat out at restaurants, and then pretend to find glass in their food. But there was a price to pay. To make their story convincing, the Evanos had to actually eat glass *before* they went to the restaurant. They munched on very finely ground glass, so it would pass through their bodies without harming them. (They hoped!) Between 1997 and 2005, the Evanos cheated insurance companies out of $200,000. They also chalked up $100,000 in unpaid hospital bills. Eventually, an insurance fraud company caught on to their scam. That's when the Evanos learned that crime (and eating glass) doesn't pay. Ronald Evano was sentenced to five years in prison. Mary got just over four years and was ordered to pay $340,000 to those she'd swindled.

PERFORMANCE EATING

In 2005, New York City artist Emily Katrencik decided that putting art in a gallery was old news. But removing something from a gallery? That would get attention. So Emily decided to eat the wall that separated the gallery's exhibition space from the gallery director's bedroom. She started gnawing on the wall a few weeks before the "exhibit" opened so there would be a hole big enough to impress visitors on opening night. Since the show lasted for a month, Emily had to eat dry wall almost every day for more than a month. She tried not to think about how eating walls might affect her health. "I look at the things in the wall that are good for me, like calcium and iron," she said.

CHUCK TAYLOR'S ALL-STARS

*Here's how those well-known Converse canvas
basketball shoes got their start.*

RAINY-DAY SHOES

When Marquis Mills Converse started a shoe company in 1908, he planned to make rubber shoes—waterproof galoshes to wear in the snow and the rain—and other work-related rubber shoes. But sales of rubber shoes were, well…seasonal. Converse needed to make money year-round, so the company turned to another season: basketball season.

Basketball had only been around for 25 years when Converse created its first shoes meant for playing the game. They were black canvas with white rubber soles or brown leather with dark rubber soles. Sales weren't bad. But they got much better when basketball player Chuck Taylor joined the Converse team.

ALL-STAR SHOES

Charles Hollis Taylor had been wearing Converse basketball shoes since 1917, during his high school years in Columbus, Indiana. Chuck wanted to be a star basketball player, and he came close. He played his first professional game in March, 1919, while still a high school student. After high school, Chuck joined the Akron Firestone Non-Skids. The Non-Skids were an "industrial league" team. Teams like the Non-Skids started the National Basketball League. In 1949—when the NBL merged with the Basketball Association of America—the NBA was born.

MR. BASKETBALL SHOES

As for Chuck Taylor, in 1921 Marquis Converse recruited the young basketball player to promote both the game and his company's shoes. Chuck brought his passion for the game to his work. He changed the shoe's design. He improved the shoe's flexibility and suggested a protective patch at the ankle. He also led the Converse company's barnstorming basketball team.

More importantly, for the company and the sport, Chuck hosted basketball "clinics" in high school and college basketball gyms across the country. Some say he almost single-handedly taught Americans the fundamentals of basketball. Before long, Chuck Taylor was more than just a Converse employee—he was "Mr. Basketball."

In 1923, Converse added Chuck Taylor's name to the All-Star logo on the ankle patch. His name became the brand name for the shoe that became synonymous with basketball. These days, Converse sneaker lovers worldwide call their favorite shoes "Chucks."

Butterflies are cannibalistic.

"HUMAN" NATURE

Turns out, people and animals have more in common than you might think.

• A group called Orangutan Outreach is giving iPads to zoos. Why? For the orangutans, of course. "We want to allow the orangutans to really play—to do paintings, to watch videos, to do almost as a human child would do with basic curiosity," said Richard Zimmerman of Orangutan Outreach. There is one problem: an organgutan can snap an iPad in half in about 15 seconds. For now, zoo keepers have to hold the tablet computers while the apes reach through the bars to use them.

• In 2012, the *Washington Post* reported that Alaskan caribou seemed to enjoy the warmth coming from the Alaska oil pipeline. "When they want to go on a date, they invite each other over to the pipeline," joked Texas Representative Louie Gohmert. Sound absurd? Oil industry experts say caribou populations have doubled since the pipeline was built. Wildlife biologists believe this could be due to climate change. Gohmert insists the pipeline brings caribou couples together.

• Imagine a robot ape being controlled by a live ape. Sci-fi? Nope. It's in the works at the Iowa Primate Learning Sanctuary in Des Moines, Iowa. Six bonobo apes (sometimes called pygmy chimpanzees) currently live at the sanctuary. For years, they've been learning to communicate with humans using a program called Bonobo Chat. Now computer science professor Ken Schweller has a working prototype of an Android app that allows the live bonobos to control a *robot* bonobo using a wireless tablet. "Controlling robots might be a good way for the bonobos to interact with visitors outside their caged areas," said Schweller. "They could play chase games or squirt guests with a water gun."

• Think pop songs are just for boy bands and screaming teens? Not so. Researchers from The University of Queensland have discovered that humpback whales love pop songs, too. All the males in a humpback whale population sing the same mating song. But, sometimes, one whale changes the song or comes up with a whole new song. Sometimes the new song includes material from the previous year's hit. "It would be like splicing an old Beatles song with U2," said researcher Ellen Garland. "Occasionally they completely throw the current song out the window and start singing a brand new song."

BATHROOM LORE

We're flush with toilet news!

IN A HURRY TO GO

In 2012, Australian stuntwoman Jolene Van Vugt set a world record. First she mounted a familiar bathroom object on a go kart. Then she sat on it, revved up, and hit the gas. What was Van Vugt driving? A motorized toilet. At the time, the record for driving a toilet was 42 mph. Van Vugt took her toilet to a record-breaking 46 mph. "I've broken Guinness World Records before, but I never thought I'd be the fastest toilet rider in the world," said Van Vugt.

PAY TOILET

Allison Berry was pulling up her pants after going to the bathroom in an Arizona restaurant when—*splash!*—her 7-carat diamond ring slipped off her finger and down the toilet. Berry was horrified. The ring was worth $70,000. It seemed like a lost cause, but plumber Mike Roberts had just the tool: a video camera with an infrared light. Roberts fished the camera down the john. He spent the next three hours scanning the pipes for shiny objects. Finally, he spotted the ring: 125 feet below the bathroom floor. To reach the ring, he would have to dig up the floor. The restaurant said yes and workers dug through the night. At 2:30 a.m. they found the ring. "We washed it off, and she put the ring back on her finger with tears of joy streaming down her cheeks," Roberts said. Cost of retrieving the ring and repairing the bathroom? Nearly $6,000.

AT ARM'S LENGTH

In 2003, a man named Edwin Gallart was on a train bound from New York City to Mount Vernon, NY. He dropped his phone into the train's john, which isn't very unusual. What is unusual? He reached down too far trying to get it back, and...he got stuck. Gallart yelled for help, but train workers couldn't free his arm. The train had to be stopped, blocking the tracks. Thousands of commuters cooled their heels while police and firefighters cut the stainless-steel toilet apart using a blowtorch. Commuter train service was snarled for hours. And...the phone was lost forever.

A LIVING TOILET

Here's one from the world of nature. *Nepenthes lowii*, a tropical pitcher plant from Borneo, survives by serving as a toilet for tree shrews. Many types of pitcher plants eat ants and other insects, but *N. lowii* lives at high elevations where there aren't enough bugs. So the plant gets much of its nutrition from shrew poop. The shrews visit the plant to eat its nectar, and while they're there they poop into the plant's open bowl. Result: plant food!

THAT'S HAIR-RAISING

What some people do with hair just might curl yours.

HAIR EXTENSIONS
Most homeowners think of metal and wood when it comes to adding an extension to their home. Not Paula Sunshine. This British craftswoman is an expert in traditional building techniques. And she

used one of those techniques—wattle and daub—to extend her thatched 16th-century home.

Wattle and daub consists of a framework of woven branches covered in plaster. It's one of the oldest known methods for building a weatherproof structure. In Britain, where Sunshine lives, traditional plaster was a mix of lime and hair. "People would use cattle hair from long-haired cattle," she said. "But we don't get many long-haired cattle around here anymore."

What *did* Sunshine use? Human hair. She collected a barrel of hair from local salons. Then she added her own hair and hair from her dogs' coats. Why hair? "The fibers hold the plaster together," said Sunshine. And because she collects freshly-shampooed hair from women's salons, her bin full of hair "smells divine."

*   *   *

MAMMOTH JOKES

Q: Why were the mammoths kicked out of the swimming pool?

A: Because they couldn't keep their trunks up.

Q: What weighs 5 tons and has 16 wheels?

A: A mammoth on roller skates.

Q: Why did the mammoth cross the road?

A: Because there weren't any chickens in the Ice Age.

100 people die each year from choking on ball-point pens.

INCREDIBLE EDIBLE BOOKS

Technically, paper is edible, but…it doesn't taste great. If you're going to eat a book, why not make it as delicious as possible?

A FOOL FOR BOOKS
To a select few people around the world, April first is more than just April Fools' Day. It's the day for an event that celebrates reading and eating: the International Edible Book Festival. "April Fools' Day is the perfect day to eat your words!" said the festival's coordinators.

The festival is fun for everyone, but some people take it very seriously. "Part of what we're trying to do is get people to stop and think about reading," said Los Angeles librarian Gary Strong. "There's nothing like feeding the tummy and the head at the same time!"

Participants make tasty artistic sculptures (usually out of cake, frosting, veggies, and fruits) of scenes or covers from their favorite books. Bibliophile (book lover) Judith A. Hoffberg got the idea for the festival at a 1999 Thanksgiving dinner with book-artist friends. Fellow artist Béatrice Coron created a website so people all over the world could participate (*www.books2eat.com*). The first festival was held in 2000, and it's been going strong ever since.

Here are a few of the most memorable edible book creations since that first festival:

Frankenstein, 2008: At the third annual Kalamazoo festival, artist Keith Jones dressed up a frankfurter as a monster and placed it in the center of a beer stein. "Frank in Stein" parodied the famous horror novel by Mary Shelley.

The Origin of Species, 2008: In 1859, biologist Charles Darwin published a book proposing the theory of evolution. A contestant at the Austin, Texas, festival decided to spoof Darwin's famous work. The entry was a mashed chocolate cake crawling with gummy worms. The title: "The Origin of Feces."

Harry Potter and the Sorcerer's Scone, 2011: A LEGO Harry Potter battled a LEGO Draco Malfoy over a tasty-looking scone at the sixth annual Edible Book Festival at Duke University in North Carolina. Attached to Harry was a paper dialogue balloon that read, "The sorcerer's scone!" Draco's speech balloon read, "Yes, and it's all mine, Harry Potter! Ha, ha, ha!"

The Hunger Games, 2012: Author Suzanne Collins's book about a world where kids face off every year in a battle to the death grew so popular that it became a blockbuster movie. Madison, Wisconsin, baker Carrie Wolfson used the book as inspiration for her entry: a blackberry pie with a mockingjay symbol made of crust. She called it "May the Odds Be Ever in Your Flavor."

RING AROUND THE CARROT

You won't believe where some lost things end up.

In 1995, Lena Paahlsson of Sweden set her wedding ring on the kitchen counter as she baked Christmas cookies. She didn't see the ring again for almost 16 years. In 2011, Lena was out in her vegetable garden, pulling up carrots. One of the carrots she yanked from the ground was wearing her missing ring. "It is quite incredible," said Lena's husband, Ola.

So how did Lena's gold-and-diamond wedding band make the journey from kitchen counter to vegetable garden? Here's what the Paahlssons believe: The ring fell into the kitchen vegetable peelings they feed to their sheep. A sheep ate the ring along with its food. The ring went through the sheep's digestive system and came out in its poop. Sheep manure was then used to fertilize the garden. And the carrot sprouted up through the ring.

*   *   *

Smell-O-Fact: American businesspeople didn't do a whole lot of research before introducing the Clairol "Mist Stick" curling iron in Germany. Since "Mist" means "manure" in German, customers weren't too eager to buy.

Dolphins have cross-shaped belly buttons.

$1 WORDS

This brain-building puzzle gives a monetary value to each letter of the alphabet. We're not telling you what those values are. But we'll give you a few clues.

Clue #1: The word "mucous" is worth 92 cents, but "snot"—though it's another word for mucous—is worth just 68 cents.

Clue #2: A single "penguin" (86 cents) is worth more than an entire "zoo" (56 cents).

Clue #3: "Math" (42 cents) is worth less than "addition" (76 cents)—but addition is just one part of math. (Huh?)

The following words are worth exactly $1. See if you can puzzle them out.

1. A synonym for cranky.

2. Something with a wattle.

3. You might set this book on them.

Still stuck? Here's a hint: The letter "j" is worth a dime. Once you know the secret, you can play around with it. How much is your name worth? Your favorite food? Can you come up with a word that's worth exactly 50 cents? Exactly $5? Is that even possible?

Answers on page 285.

Only state never to have been ruled at some point by another country: Idaho.

TAKE A BITE

As weird as it sounds, there's a word for eating poo:
coprophagy. And you won't believe who's doing it.

DUNG BEETLES DO IT

Dung beetles can be found all over the world, in deserts, forests, pastures...everywhere that poo can be found. That's because poo is their life. Some roll it up into balls. Some bury it in their tunnels. Others live in piles of it. But all of them eat it, and they even have favorite kinds. Most prefer dung from herbivores (plant eaters). When a plant eater chews, swallows, and digests, parts of the plants pass through undigested. The undigested bits pass out of the animal in its dung and offer the nutrition dung beetles need. Adult dung beetles even feed poo to their larvae. In parts of Texas, dung beetles and their young consume up to 80 percent of the cow pies cattle leave behind.

COMMON BLUE BUTTERFLIES DO IT

They look like fluttering blue angels as they fly from stop to stop, drinking nectar from flowers and laying eggs on the leaves that surround them. But now and then, they've been spotted drinking something stomach-turning: the liquids in fresh dog poo. Seems fresh poo can be filled with nutrients, including minerals not digested as they went through the dog's system.

CATTLE DO IT

When chickens poop, they flush out protein their bodies didn't digest. That calorie-rich poo is then mixed with grain and fed to cattle. Heating the recycled poo to 160 degrees Fahrenheit is supposed to make it safe for cattle to eat. But many experts link feeding chicken litter to cattle with mad-cow disease. Chicken poo as a livestock-feed supplement has been banned in many countries, including Canada and Great Britain, but, so far, the U.S. has not banned the practice.

RABBITS DO IT

Rabbits eat hay, vegetables, fruit, dandelions, and other wild weeds. They digest their food and eliminate the waste like other mammals. But almost as soon as their soft poo pellets (called *cecotropes*) hit the ground, rabbits eat them. Eating the fresh pellets guarantees that the rabbit will have plenty of vitamin B12 and other crucial nutrients. But rabbits do have some standards. When they poop a second time, they don't eat their droppings.

ELEPHANTS DO IT

Baby elephants drink their mothers' milk, as do all mammals. But they get an important digestive aid from Mom by eating her poop. Most animals—especially

The Hot Wheels version of the 1968 Corvette was in stores before the real thing was available.

those that eat plants—need an array of bacteria in their bodies to properly digest their food. Newborn elephants don't have these important bacteria. The best source of the bacteria they need? Mother's fresh feces.

CHIMPANZEES DO IT

Scientist Tetsuya Sakamaki of the Primate Research Institute in Japan studies chimpanzees. What she's discovered: When food is scarce, chimps eat their own poop. Sakamaki called the practice an "adaptive feeding strategy." By eating poop, chimpanzees get the nutrients their digestive systems might have missed the first time around. During her study, at least five female chimps ate and inspected their own poo to gather discarded *Dialium* seeds, which are rich in protein.

DOGS DO IT

Dogs are *canids*, believed to be descended from wild wolves tens—or even hundreds—of thousands of years ago. Canids are *carnivores*—meat eaters. Throughout their long history, they have been a very successful species of animal for one key reason: They are also opportunistic eaters. That means they eat whatever they can find. Throughout the dog's lengthy history, if food was scarce, eating poop helped them survive until they could hunt again. Your household pet is probably never that hungry. But from time to time, when something is missing from a pet dog's diet, the old instinct kicks in, and it will eat its scat, or even the scat of another dog.

WHOSE NOSE?

Schnoz, beak, honker, conk...whatever you call these animal noses, they're tough to ignore. See if you can match each nose to its owner.

THIS NOSE...

1. is bright blue and red and matches the animal's rear end.

2. has 300 million scent receptors to track with.

3. probably can't smell a thing because the animal has no olfactory lobes in its brain.

4. can be inflated to scare away the competition.

5. can grip like a hand.

6. has 22 pink tentacles.

7. detects food electrically like a metal detector finds coins on a beach.

8. can be seven inches long and is blown like a horn to attract females.

9. contains a magnet that helps guide it home.

10. sneezes when it rains.

BELONGS TO A...

a. tapir

b. star-nosed mole

c. mandrill

d. dolphin

e. dog

f. elephant seal

g. proboscis monkey

h. elephantnose fish

i. snub-nosed monkey

j. homing pigeon.

Answers on page 286.

An earthworm has five hearts.

FAFROTSKIES

Stories of animals raining from the sky have been around for thousands of years. They even show up in holy writings. The phenomenon is called "fafrotskies" (for "falling from the skies"). Here are some of our favorite reports.

FALLING FISH DOWN-UNDER

Christine Balmer was afraid her family would think she'd lost her mind if she told them she'd seen fish raining from the sky. Luckily for Balmer, she was not alone. Dozens of other people living in Lajamanu, Australia, also saw the fish fall in 2010. When it stopped, small, dead, spangled perch were scattered all over the city. "These fish were alive when they hit the ground," said Balmer.

It wasn't the first time Lajamanu had been pelted with fish. Similar reports were filed in 1974 and again in 2004. Why Lajamanu? The nearest lakes are hundreds of miles from the city. Still, weather experts admit that if a tornado hit either lake, the updraft could form a waterspout 60,000 to 70,000 feet high. And that waterspout might include schools of fish.

"Once the fish get up into the weather system, they are pretty much frozen. After some time, they're released," said Mark Kersemaker from the Australian Bureau of Meteorology. And—*splash!*—it's raining fish.

"Thank God it didn't rain crocodiles," said Balmer.

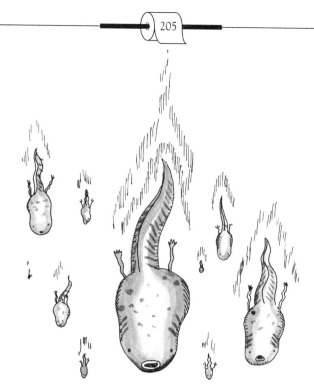

TADPOLES OVER ISHIKAWA

In June of 2009, startled people all over Japan's Ishikawa Prefecture called local officials with a bizarre story: Dead tadpoles were falling from the sky. One 55-year-old witness said he heard something strange from the parking lot of the Nanao city civic center. When he went outside to check, he discovered dead tadpoles covering dozens of car windshields. Forty-eight hours later, a similar report of dead tadpoles came in from Hakusan, a few miles away.

Some experts suggested a flock of birds must have flown over and spit the tadpoles onto the cars below. But officials at the Yamashina Institute for Ornithology dismissed the suggestion. "Crows eat tadpoles. But if

these were spat out by birds, a wider area should have
been covered."

KENTUCKY MEAT SHOWER

On a cloudless day in March of 1876 , Mrs. Allen
Crouch was making soap in the yard of her Kentucky
farm. Something started to fall from the sky. The
"something" turned out to be tiny flakes of raw meat.

Within ten minutes, enough meat to fill a horse
wagon had covered an area about 100 by 50 yards in
size. Two men who wandered by offered to taste the
meat and claimed it was either mutton or venison. But
other theories quickly flew through the nearby town of
Olympian Springs.

Professor Lawrence Smith of Louisville said the meat
was the "dried spawn of babeachian reptiles" (his weird
way of saying *frogs*). Author William Livingston Alden
believed the flakes were fragments of alien beings,
pulverized by the explosion of their distant home planet.

Dr. L.D. Kastenbine, a local professor of chemistry,
supported the venison theory. The most logical
explanation, he claimed, was that a large flock of
vultures had gorged themselves on a dead deer. As they
flew over the Crouch farm, something startled the birds.
And they vomited the contents of their over-filled
stomachs all over Mrs. Crouch.

To read about more odd things that fall from the sky,
turn to page 246.

MONSTER QUOTES

Monsters might not live under your bed or in your closet, but that doesn't stop people from talking about them.

"The piano is a monster that screams when you touch its teeth."

—**Andrés Segovia (classical guitarist)**

"I am able to play monsters well. I understand monsters."

—**Anthony Hopkins (actor)**

"Imagination creates some big monsters."

—**Olivier Martinez (French actor)**

"Godzilla's a monster for the '90s. He's been working out!"

—**Hank Azaria (actor)**

"I left Ohio when I was 17 and ended up in New York and realized that not all films had giant crab monsters in them. It really opened up a lot of things for me."

—**Jim Jarmusch (filmmaker)**

"The artist must bow to the monster of his own imagination."

—**Richard Wright (author)**

"When I was nine I played the demon king in Cinderella. It launched me on a long and happy life of being a monster."

—**Boris Karloff (actor)**

Of the 12 men who have walked on the moon, 11 were Boy Scouts.

CHILD PRODIGIES

If you're like Uncle John, it takes you years of practice to get good at something. But some kids seem to be born geniuses. And no one knows why.

NANCY YI FAN, CHILD NOVELIST

Nancy Yi Fan and her family moved from China to the United States in 2000. Nancy was seven years old. Before the move, she spoke almost no English. But she quickly mastered the language by reading dozens of books. Reading inspired Nancy to write. She completed her first fantasy novel, *Swordbird*, when she was eleven years old. It was published two years later by HarperCollins. The book is about blue jays warring against cardinals and a heroic bird who rescues them from the evil machinations of the tyrant hawk lord. Nancy's love of birds helped her create the story, and she made the book's fight scenes feel real by studying kung fu.

"All the other kids out there...follow your dreams," Nancy has said. "Truly, nothing is impossible."

LILLY GASKIN, CHILD GEOGRAPHER

In 2007, Oprah Winfrey introduced the world to Provo, Utah, geography whiz Lilly Gaskin on her talk show. Lilly was two years old at the time. She had started studying world geography at 16 months when her favorite uncle went to Taiwan. Lilly's parents showed her where the country was on a map. The next time she saw the map, she remembered the country's name and its location. Impressed by her memory of Taiwan, Lilly's grandfather showed her a second country on the map. She memorized its location, too. In no time, Lilly could find more than 100 countries on a world map.

AKRIT JASWAL, CHILD SURGEON

India-born Akrit Jaswal could hold a conversation by the time he was ten months old. By age two, he could read. By the time he was seven years old—when most kids are starting second grade—Akrit was performing his first surgery. He repaired the hands of a young burn victim who was just a year older than himself. Akrit was not yet a licensed doctor, but locally he was known as a "medical genius." The operation was a roaring success.

At age 13, Akrit was named one of India's smartest people (his IQ measured 146—genius level). At age 17, Akrit was working on a master's degree in applied chemistry. He believes he is on the verge of finding a cure for cancer. And he dreams of bringing dinosaurs back from extinction.

...in the Fenway Park crowd scene in *Field of Dreams.*

DIGEST THIS

You might be surprised by what some animals (and plants) have to do to get a square meal.

MOON SNAILS

If you've ever picked up a clamshell and seen a hole that looks like it's been made by an electric drill, you've seen the work of a moon snail. These hungry sea snails are members of the mollusk family. And they prey on other mollusks—usually clams. Moon snails drill those perfect holes with a body part called a *radula* (picture a tongue with teeth). Once the hole has been drilled, the moon snail injects a digestive acid into the hole. And—*presto, chango!*—liquid clam. The moon snail slurps the liquefied clam up through the hole. An adult moon snail, the top predator where oceans meet beaches, can eat a clam every four days.

HAMMERHEAD FLATWORMS

The hammerhead flatworm is native to Indo-China but spread around the world in the soil of greenhouse plants. It's an invasive pest that hunts along a trail of its own slime. The flatworm's favorite meal? Earthworms. It oozes through the soil until it catches up with an earthworm. Then it pushes its jaws outside its mouth and latches onto the worm. Next it releases an enzyme

Below -90 degrees F, your breath will freeze in the air and fall to the ground.

that dissolves the earthworm's body, and slurps down its liquefied meal.

CAMEL SPIDERS

The camel spider—also called a wind scorpion—isn't a true spider. It isn't a scorpion either (or a camel for that matter). But it does look a bit like a cross between a scorpion and a tarantula with horrifyingly huge jaws. Camel spiders can grow to be 6 inches around (bigger than a teacup). But size is only part of what makes these predators found in northern Africa and the Middle East so deadly. The other parts? Camel spiders can run up to 10 miles per hour, about a third as fast as the swiftest human runner. So they have no problem outrunning prey—other insects, lizards, rodents, and even birds. And then...there are those jaws. A camel spider's jaws can make up one-third of its total body length. Once a camel spider catches something, it uses those powerful jaws (called *chelicerae*) to seize the victim and chop it to bits like some insect food processor. As if that's not enough, the camel spider has digestive fluids that then liquefy its victim's flesh so it can suck what's left of its meal into its stomach.

*   *   *

Smell-O-Fact: The first known landfill opened in Athens, Greece, around 500 B.C.E. By law, it had to be two miles outside the city. Why? Because trash had previously been piled outside the city walls. That made it easy for invaders to climb up the garbage and enter the city.

Survey says: 10 percent of Brits put their underwear in the refrigerator to help stay cool.

COMIC GENIUSES

More stories about how famous cartoonists got their start.
(See "Meet Weenie Man" on page 62.)

COMIC GENIUS: Chester Gould
FAMOUS COMIC STRIP: *Dick Tracy*
HOW IT ALL BEGAN: In 1921, twenty-year-old Chester Gould moved to Chicago, hoping to find success as a cartoonist. He had a long wait. For ten years, he stocked shelves at an A&P grocery store to pay the bills. In his spare time, he came up with ideas for comic strips. He sent more than 60 different strips to editors at Chicago's six daily newspapers. They featured characters such as "the beautiful girl," "the office boy," "the smart aleck," and "the oddball." None of them clicked.

The problem? Gould was trying to be funny, and there were a lot of cartoonists trying to do the same thing. Then he got an idea. In the 1930s, Chicago was overrun with gangsters. They sold alcohol illegally, ran gambling rings and other rackets, and killed their rivals with machine guns. And most of the time, they got away with it!

"A known gangster would be arrested in the morning, and late that afternoon, he'd be back out on the streets,"

Gould said. He blamed corrupt judges and police officers who looked the other way. Chicago needed "A symbol of law and order who could 'dish it out' to the underworld exactly as they dished it out—only better," Gould said. If the real authorities weren't doing their jobs, then maybe Gould could create a comic strip detective that would.

Gould invented Dick Tracy, an undercover detective who was tougher than the gangsters. The founder of the *New York Daily News* loved the strip. He published the first strip in 1931 in the *Detroit Mirror*, then in the *News*. Soon it was picked up by papers nationwide.

Dick Tracy was one of the first "story strips," with a continuing saga. Humor strips ended with a joke and didn't usually build on a story from day to day. But *Dick Tracy* built suspense, so readers didn't want to miss a single day.

COMIC GENIUS: Charles M. Schulz
FAMOUS COMIC STRIP: *Peanuts*
HOW IT ALL BEGAN: Charles M. Schulz never considered himself normal. He was small and felt overlooked by everyone. So he would go home after school and invent characters like Little Julius (named after the Roman emporer Julius Caesar), who was a small but powerful kid.

Schulz discovered that he was very good at drawing. He'd imitate the comic strips he saw in the newspaper, especially *Buck Rogers in the 25th Century AD* and

Superman. Other kids asked him to draw pictures of Disney's Mickey Mouse or the Three Little Pigs on their notebooks. He liked the attention that brought him, and he wanted to create his own characters.

As an adult, his first cartoon was called *Li'l Folks*, and it appeared in the June 8, 1947, edition of the *Minneapolis Star-Tribune*. The cartoon shows a young boy with two pairs of boxing gloves. He's standing by a girl, who's sitting on a couch and showing no interest. The boy is saying, "Oh, rats, you never want to do anything."

In 1950, when the United Features Syndicate began distributing the strip to newspapers across the country, *Li'l Folks* was renamed *Peanuts.* As for how he created one of the most popular comic strips of all time, Schulz said, "A normal person couldn't do it."

A HANDFUL OF PEANUTS TRIVIA

• Schulz's nickname as a kid was "Sparky." He signed his early *Li'l Folks* cartoons with that name.

• Schulz did not like the name *Peanuts*, but United Features insisted on the name change. "*Peanuts* is the worst title ever thought up for a comic strip," he said.

• Snoopy is based on Schulz's childhood dog, Spike, who was very independent.

• Schulz published 17,897 *Peanuts* strips. Some successful cartoonists hire other artists to help, but Scultz wrote and illustrated every one of his strips.

RAT-PATOOTIE

More cartoon character quotes.

Rapunzel: "Something brought you here, Flynn Rider. Call it what you will…fate…destiny…"
Flynn Rider: "A horse."

—*Tangled*

"The Sword of Heroes! Said to be so sharp you can get cut just by looking at…Ow!"
—Po, *Kung Fu Panda*

"(To Hiccup) Don't worry. You're small and you're weak. That'll make you less of a target! The dragons will see you as sick or insane and go after the more Viking-like teens instead."

—Gobber, *How To Train Your Dragon*

Jill: "Is it true, a cat always lands on its feet?"
Puss in Boots: "No! That is just a rumor spread by dogs!"

—*Puss in Boots*

"No matter how many times you save the world, it always manages to get back in jeopardy again."
—Mr. Incredible, *The Incredibles*

"If you're gonna name a food, you should give it a name that sounds delicious. Ratatouille doesn't sound delicious. It sounds like 'rat' and 'patootie.' 'Rat-patootie,' which does not sound delicious."

—Linguini, *Ratatouille*

MAKE A DOWSING STICK

The next time you're searching for treasure, why not make yourself a dowsing stick? Oldtimers swear by them.

STICK A FORK IN IT

Dowsers use their dowsing sticks (also called "witching rods" or "doodlebugs") to find groundwater, gems, jewels, money, and other underground treasures. Some dowsers

even use their sticks to communicate with spirits and predict the future. Skeptics swear the sticks don't work, but many a well brimming with water has been dug after a dowser has located just the right spot.

There isn't really much "making" involved with a dowsing stick—you just need to do some hunting. Ideally, you want to find a forked (Y-shaped) stick with two "tines" that are long enough to hold. The handles of the forked stick should be between one and two feet long. The stick also has to be bendable rather than stiff. If your stick has any sharp or pointy bits on it, nag a grown-up into sawing them off for you.

HOW TO DOWSE: METHOD 1

Start by lightly grasping the "tines" of your stick with your palms up. Keep the stick parallel to the ground or tilted slightly upward. Either take the stick to an area where you feel something is hidden or just walk with it over places you normally go. When an object is underfoot, the dowsing stick may pull downward or begin to twitch. One dowser describes an up-and-down movement, "almost as if the stick has a life of its own."

HOW TO DOWSE: METHOD 2

If your parents don't want you digging up the yard, use your dowsing stick to answer questions or predict the future. Write all the letters of the alphabet on a large sheet of paper (big letters may work better). Hold your stick over the paper, and ask a question out loud. Focus on the question and see if the stick seems to lead you to spell out words. Or, instead of the alphabet, jot down words, names, numbers, or "yes" and "no" answers.

Does dowsing really work? Dowsers say they have proof: they find what they're looking for. *The Skeptic's Dictionary* calls that *post hoc reasoning*. (Huh?) That's short for the Latin phrase *post hoc, ergo propter hoc*: "After this, therefore because of this." Post hoc reasoning works like this: You find a four-leaf clover and put it in your math book. Then you make an "A" on your math test. You decide that the "lucky" clover helped you get a good grade, simply because you found it before the test. Scientists call that "false logic."

IT CAME FROM... JAPAN!

What do a blue plastic box, a soccer ball, and a fishing vessel have in common? Here's the story.

SWEPT AWAY

On March 11, 2011, a monster tsunami scoured away entire towns along the coast of Japan. The disaster claimed nearly 19,000 lives. According to the Japanese government, the giant sea wave left behind 25 million tons of rubble. No one knows exactly how much of it ended up in the water, but it's estimated to be around 5 million tons.

All those floaters had to go somewhere. As it turns out, some of the rubble is making the 5,000 mile voyage across the Pacific Ocean to the United States. How much? About 1.5 million tons.

Height of Mt. Olympus on planet Mars: 15 miles.

TRACKING TRAGEDY

The National Oceanic and Atmospheric Administration (NOAA) is leading the drive to predict the number and type of items that may wash ashore. And they've invited the public to help. As part of a NOAA shoreline monitoring project, volunteers will collect information on the types and amounts of debris on U.S. shores for two years. They've also set up a Tsunami Debris Hotline number: 2-1-1.

Some predictions are grim. Nearly two years after the tsunami, 2,184 people were still missing. Curtis Ebbesmeyer, an oceanographer who tracks flotsam, fears West Coast beachcombers could find floating shoes with human remains still inside. "We're expecting one hundred sneakers," he said. Ebbesmeyer stressed how important it is to treat such items with respect. "They may be the only remains that a Japanese family will ever have of people that were lost," he said.

LOST AND FOUND

Experts say debris will continue to find its way to the U.S. for years to come. These items have been confirmed by NOAA as having floated from Japan.

FLOATER: A boxcar-sized dock
FOUND ON: June 5, 2012
STORY: After its long trip across the Pacific, a Japanese dock floated ashore on Agate Beach near Newport, Oregon. It did not come alone. Hundreds of millions of

marine organisms hitched a ride. Some of those species have officials worried, including a tiny species of crab, a species of algae, and a little starfish, all native to Japan. West Coast biologists identified one hitchhiker as a marine algae native to Japan known as *wakame* (wah-KAH-may). It's a kind of kelp, and it's on the list of the "World's Worst Invasive Species." What makes wakame so scary? Environmental biologists say it "harms native kelp, mucks up marinas and the undersides of boats, and damages oyster farming." It also rots and makes beaches smell so bad swimmers avoid them.

FLOATER: 164-foot fishing vessel
FOUND ON: March 20, 2012
STORY: The rusted-out fishing vessel *Ryou-Un Maru* was destined for the scrap heap when the tsunami knocked it away from its mooring in Hokkaido, Japan. The ship drifted all the way across the Pacific and ended up in the Gulf of Alaska. The U.S. Coast Guard decided the derelict was a danger to shipping and a threat to the state's coastline. So they sank it.

FLOATER: A soccer ball
FOUND IN: March, 2012
STORY: 16-year-old Misaki Murakami lost his home along with all the furniture, toys, and keepsakes inside it to the 2011 tsunami. He thought he'd never see any of those things again. That was before David Baxter went beachcombing on Middleton Island, south of the Alaskan mainland. What he found: a soccer ball. And

not just any soccer ball. This one had writing on it. It was given to Misaki in 2005. He was in third grade at the time, and his classmates gave the ball to him as a good-bye gift when he transferred to another school. The ball had his name written on it, along with messages of encouragement. Baxter's wife is Japanese, so she was able to call Misaki to tell him the good news. "I've lost everything in the tsunami. So I'm delighted," he said. "I really want to say thank you for finding the ball."

OTHER FLOATERS

• A small, barnacle-crusted fishing boat floundered facedown at the edge of the beach in Cape Disappointment, Washington.

• A basketball found by cleanup workers near Craig, Alaska, had the words "Kesen chu" written on it. That's short for Kesennuma Chugakko (Kesennuma Middle School). Kesennuma is a fishing port hit hard by the tsunami.

• About 400 Japanese fishing buoys have floated across the Pacific to Alaska, British Columbia, Washington, and Oregon.

• A 170-ft. squid-fishing boat ended up in British Columbia's coastal waters.

• A Harley-Davidson motorcycle with Japanese license plates made it to British Columbia's Graham Islands in a foam-lined container.

BRAIN CONTROL

Attention, computer geeks and gamers! The future isn't right around the corner. It's strapped around your forehead.

E LECTRIC MINDS
In 2012, a *Scientific American* columnist announced the "dawn of the brain-computer interface." BCI means the end of keyboards, computer mice, touch screens, and voice recognition. It means the time has come to control your games and gadgets with (*bwa-ha-ha…*) your brain.

The human brain is made up of billions of neurons about the size of a pinhead. All those teeny neurons are interconnected. Every connection between neurons creates a tiny electrical discharge, measurable by EEG (electroencephalogram) machines. And EEG tech is what drives today's BCI.

Reports warn that early BCI products are pretty crude. But it won't be long before all you have to do is think about what you want your gadget to do, and "poof"—your wish is its command. Until that happens, here's the latest in brain-control fun.

THE TOY: *Star Wars Science Force Trainer* (Uncle Milton)
The trainer comes with a wireless headset and a ping-pong ball in a clear plastic tube. There's a fan beneath the tube.

WHAT IT DOES: Puts your Jedi skills to the test. As you control your thoughts, the ball moves up the tube.
HOW IT WORKS: The Force Trainer uses EEG technology to track the brain's electrical impulses. It reads your brain's (relaxed) alpha brain waves and (focused) beta waves. As you focus your thoughts, your brain activity revs up the fan and the ping-pong ball rises up the tube. Fun extra: Yoda's voice comes out of the toy to guide you: "Do or do not; there is no try."

THE TOY: *Mindflex Duel* (Mattel)
This is another ball-in-the-air with a fan and wireless headsets. For extra fun, the headsets have dangling clips that attach to your ears.
WHAT IT DOES: Allows a mind battle between friends (or archenemies). Kind of like tug-of-war, but with a tiny foam ball, using brains instead of brawn.
HOW IT WORKS: This one uses EEG tech, too. Mattel claims that it reads the low-level brain waves

and speeds up or slows down the fan to keep the ball in the air. Players guide the ball through a cannon, basket, flip frame, and wind wheel. The fan power controls the height of the ball, and focused beta brain waves control the fan power.

MATTEL'S MIND-CONTROL TIPS

- Relax the muscles in your face.
- Stare at the ball and focus all your attention on it.
- Picture the ball rising.
- Focus on the exact spot you want the ball to reach.
- Imagine pushing the ball up with your mind.
- Do math problems in your head.
- Think the same thought over and over.

THE TOY: *MindWave Mobile Headset* (NeuroSky)
WHAT IT DOES: Allows players to control games. The "MindHunter" game requires sharp focus and eye blinks to fire a slingshot, crossbow, or shotgun at innocent-looking animals like sheep and rabbits. "MindLabyrinth" goes in the opposite direction. Players must relax enough to sink through 52 levels and reach Pachamama's Hidden Temple.
HOW IT WORKS: Once again, EEG technology powers the game. The headset measures the brain's electrical impulses in the forehead. And the sensor in this one also detects muscle movements, such as eye blinks. A chip converts signals from analog format to digital. And signals then travel wirelessly to a computer.

CAT GOT YOUR TONGUE?

Ever think about how many words and expressions have "cat" in them? We did.

Caterwaul: to screech or howl like a fighting cat.

Catastrophe: an event causing great damage and suffering.

Fat cat: a wealthy person; someone who lives life like a pampered cat.

Catlap: tea so weak it's only fit for cats to drink.

Cattail: a tall marsh plant with brown furry spikes.

Playing cat and mouse: to torment someone weaker in a playful manner.

Like herding cats: an impossible task.

Catcall: booing bad acting. In Shakespeare's time, people yowled actors off the stage by making a racket like cats howling on a fence.

When the cat's away, the mice will play: without supervision, people get into mischief.

Catwalk: a narrow walkway. Comes from a cat's ability to balance and walk on just about anything.

WHAT'S IN YOUR LOCKER?

*Here's a kid who dared to lend books to her friends.
What makes that so special? All of the books had been
banned from her school library.*

CODE NAME: RULE BREAKER

In 2008, a student who goes by the name Nekochan started a covert lending library out of her school locker. The undercover librarian was a student at a Catholic high school somewhere in the U.S. Her school had released a lo-o-ng list of books students would not be allowed to read. Many of the books listed were among her favorites. Plenty of others were literary classics, books that had weathered the test of time and been judged by experts as among the best literature ever written. "One of my personal favorites, *Catcher in the Rye*, was on the list," Nekochan wrote, "so I decided to bring it to school to see if I would really get in trouble."

CATCH 'ER ON THE SLY

Nekochan's defiant act caught the eye of a fellow student. A boy in her English class had heard that *Catcher in the Rye* was a great read. He knew that it had been banned, and that made him even more interested. Nekochan loaned him the book. Word got around, and other students asked to borrow books. Soon, her locker was overflowing with banned books.

TROUBLING TALES

Nekochan chose the books for her "secret" library based on literary quality. Stuffed inside her locker-library were treasures such as these, plus a lot more:

The Hunger Games by Suzanne Collins
The Canterbury Tales by Geoffrey Chaucer
His Dark Materials trilogy by Philip Pullman
A Connecticut Yankee in King Arthur's Court by Mark Twain
Sabriel by Garth Nix
The Divine Comedy by Dante Alighieri
Slaughterhouse-Five by Kurt Vonnegut
Lord of the Flies by William Golding
Bridge to Terabithia by Katherine Paterson
The Perks of Being a Wallflower by Stephen Chbosky
The Hitchhiker's Guide to the Galaxy by Douglas Adams
Paradise Lost by John Milton
Animal Farm by George Orwell
The Witches by Roald Dahl

Read them if you dare!

EXTREME EXOPLANETS

Powerful telescopes now allow scientists to gaze into the cosmos. More than 1,000 exoplanets have been discovered. Here are three extreme examples.

PLANET HD 80606B

200 light years from Earth in the constellation Ursa Major (the Big Bear), this giant ball of gas is so hot it glows red. It has 4 times the mass of Jupiter, the biggest planet in our solar system, and an elliptical (egg-shaped) orbit. It swings around its sun every 111.4 Earth days. And as it gets closer to that sun, the gas giant's temperature goes up by 700 degrees. Surface temperatures soar to 1230 degrees Celsius (2246°F). That's hotter than molten lava. And that's not all—the rise in temperature creates explosive fire storms. Fiery winds travel from the planet's day side to its night side at 3 miles a second, faster than the speed of sound.

TRES-2B

750 light years away in the constellation Draco (the dragon) is a gas giant that orbits really really close to its star. How close? So close that its atmosphere reaches temperatures of 1000 degrees Celsius (1800°F). But here's what has scientists puzzled: TrES-2b is dark. It reflects less light than if it had been painted with

black acrylic paint. In fact, its atmopshere seems to be absorbing light. Scientists have detected the presence of light-absorbing chemicals like vaporized sodium and potassium or titanium oxide in the planet's atmosphere. But that doesn't explain why the planet is darker than any planet or moon in our own solar system. "It's not clear what is responsible for making this planet so extraordinarily dark," said David Spiegel of Princeton University. But…it's not totally dark. TrES-2b is so hot that it glows red, like the burner on an electric stove.

PSR J1719-1438

Orbiting a *pulsar* (a neutron star that emits rapid pulses of radiation) 4000 light years away in the constellation Serpens, (the snake) this exoplanet is a true "gem." It not only has a super-fast orbit of only 2 hours and 10 minutes, but probably started off life as a "white dwarf" star. Over the eons, its gaseous outer layers were stripped away by the gravity from the pulsar. What's left? Nothing but its carbon and oxygen center—a center that has crystallized into a *diamond* 5 times the size of Earth.

*   *   *

THE SIDESHOW STUNTMAN

Want to give your parents nightmares? Tell them you plan to be just like this guy when you grow up!

TOO MUCH LIKE WORK

Sideshow performer Preacher Muad'dib doesn't have a "real job." He spends his days breathing fire, throwing knives, and balancing things like lawn mowers on his face.

As a kid, Preacher wanted to be a magician. "I used to drive my parents nuts with it," he said. "I was a nightmare. Finally, in an attempt to make me disappear, my dad bought me a magic set."

It only took a few minutes of messing around with props to convince Preacher that magic wasn't all it was cracked up to be. "Magic is too much hard work," he said. "I am a lazy, lazy man. So I learned sideshow stunts instead. It's the same as magic, but it's all real—no tricks!"

THAT'S EXTREME

These days, Preacher performs with friends at Circa Extreme. The circus includes fire breathers, fire dancers, stilt walkers, trapeze artists, and poi spinners. Poi spinning is an art that originated with the Maori people in New Zealand. It involves swinging weighted balls (that may or may not be on fire) from strings on your fingers.

Preacher specializes in acts most people think are insane, like eating a handful of glass or sticking a power drill up his nose. Like everyone else, you may be wondering: What's the worst thing to have ever gone wrong during one of Preacher's performances. Well… according to Preacher, the *real* trick is pulling off his stunts without getting hurt.

"Everything we do is real—real nails, real drills, real chainsaws," he said. But according to Preacher, the whole point is to do all these things that people say can't be done *without* hurting yourself. "If you can only do it by hurting yourself, then you can't do it!"

FLAME ON!

Over the years, Preacher has gotten good enough at risking his life to rack up a handful of world records. Most recently, he snagged the 2012 record for "Most Flames Blown in One Minute." To break the record, he blew 69 fire torches from his mouth, one after the other. And he did it in 60 seconds during an outdoor performance in London. In another show, he managed to blow 83 flames in the same amount of time. Preacher also holds records for the most spins of a fire staff in one minute (150) and the longest time balancing a fire staff on his tongue (16 seconds).

But Preacher's most interesting world record might be the one he holds for balancing a lawnmower on his face. He performed the stunt onstage, starting in a kneeling position. After lifting the handle of the mower to his chin, he took his hands away and swayed gently from side to side to keep the mower balanced, always looking straight above at the blades. After 40 seconds on his knees, he rose to a standing position, still keeping the mower balanced. He was able to keep standing for another 31 seconds, breaking the world record with a final time of 71 seconds. That was right before he doubled over and clutched his chin in pain.

When Preacher performs the stunt without trying to break a record, he lets audience members throw heads of lettuce into the spinning mower blades, calling the trick the "Lawnmower of Doom."

"It's a preposterous thing to do, and it took a lot of practice!" Preacher warned.

In other words, kiddies...don't try this stuff at home (or your parents won't just have nightmares, they'll have hospital bills).

NO TIME LIKE THE PRESENT

Most physicists believe that time is not a straight line from past to present to future. Past, present, and future are all present, all of the time. Here's why.

Real ideas about time travel start with Albert Einstein's Special Theory of Relativity. The theory says that the faster you travel through *space*, the slower you travel through *time*. If you hop a plane from New York to London, traveling at, say, 500 mph, by the time you get home, you'd be about 30 nanoseconds younger than the brother you left behind. Neither of you would notice, of course. But if you could travel through space at the speed of light for 10 years, by the time you returned, your brother (and everyone else you knew and loved) would be long dead. Why? Because a thousand years would have passed. Your "present" and your brother's "present" would now be...1,000 years apart.

Einstein didn't stop with his first theory. His second theory—on general relativity—says that space-time can be bent. One point in time can be bent to touch any other long-past or far-future moment. Kind of like stretching a Gumby toy so that its bendy green head touches its bendy green toes. If the past can touch the present, is it still the past or is it now the present?

THE BRAIN MUSEUM

Who wouldn't love to have a collection of brains in jars?

JARHEADS

In 1889, college professor Burt Green Wilder founded the Cornell Brain Society. Then he started collecting brains. By 1925, Wilder had amassed at least 600—possibly 1,000—of them. When he died that year, the collection added one more: his.

No one showed much interest in the collection after Dr. Wilder died. The brains were kept in jars of formaldehyde, a chemical that's good for preserving things. They were left in a basement at Cornell University, and time took its toll. When the university decided to display the brains—after 50 years in storage—only about 70 were worth keeping.

GREEN GIANT

One of the most interesting brains that remains once belonged to Edward Rulloff. Rulloff was the last person legally hanged in the state of New York. In 1871, he was convicted of murdering his wife and child. His unusually large brain is greener than the others in the collection. "It's a nice peppermint color," says Dr. Barbara L. Finlay, who's now in charge of the brain collection.

LIBERATED BRAINS

The collection also includes the cranial remains of Helen Hamilton Gardener, a famous writer known to be a very smart lady. It seems Dr. Wilder believed that men had superior brains. "He was a little misguided," said Supriya Syal, who helps manage the brain collection. "He assumed that the brains of educated men would be different from those of women, criminals, and the mentally challenged." Gardener had her brain delivered to Cornell after her death—to prove that women's brains were not inferior to men's in any way.

GRAY MATTERS

Wilder hoped that studying brains would reveal why humans differ so much. Some are geniuses, others not very bright. Many are kind, but some are criminals. Wilder thought he would find major differences in size, shape, and weight between the brains of "educated and orderly persons" and those of women, murderers, racial minorities, and the mentally ill.

What he found: the differences—if there were any—could not be detected. Most brains were quite similar. They looked like gray hunks of rubber. As for Wilder's brain? It looks like all the others, floating in its jar.

*   *   *

AND THE WINNER IS...

Human actors win golden Oscar statues at the Academy Awards. But canine stars? They go for golden collars!

GO FOR THE GOLD

On February 13, 2012, four-legged actors and their two-legged owners and fans packed the Egyptian Theater in Los Angeles for the first annual Golden Collar awards. The awards celebrated dogs in movies and television. Barks and applause filled the theater as the winners were announced in five categories: Best Dog in a Theatrical Film, Best Dog in a Foreign Film, Best Dog in a Television Series, Best Dog in a Reality Series, and Best Dog in a Direct-to-DVD Film.

The nominees, dressed in tuxedos and red bow ties, seemed oblivious to the ceremony. Blackie, the Doberman nominated for his role in Martin Scorcese's 3D blockbuster movie, *Hugo*, couldn't attend. And his two Doberman stand-ins snoozed right through the awards. (Of course, their noses perked up at the end when bags of doggie treats made the rounds.)

Winners trotted home with trophies that featured a gem-studded Italian leather collar on a paw-shaped Plexiglas stand. And now, on with the awards!

Claude Monet (1840–1926) painted more than 300 pictures of...

YOUR GOLDEN COLLAR AWARD WINNERS...

Best Dog in a Theatrical Film: Uggie

Starring in: *The Artist*

Uggie, the scene-stealing Jack Russell terrier in *The Artist*, won paws down for the Best Dog in a Theatrical Film. Uggie faced stiff competition from Blackie, the Doberman Pinscher star of *Hugo*, directed by Martin Scorsese. But Scorsese's plug for the Dobie in the *Los Angles Times* didn't sway the judges. Nor did a write-in campaign for Blackie on Facebook. After winning his golden collar, Uggie turned up at the Oscars in a satin bowtie with an 18-carat-gold doggie bone. He got to show off his garb on stage when *The Artist* won the Oscar for Best Picture.

Best Dog in a Foreign Film: Koko

Starring in: *Red Dog* (Australian film)

For Koko's audition, the director asked the Kelpie to look "sad, "confused," and then "angry," all on cue. Not on cue, Koko appeared mortified when he learned that his brown coat would be dyed red for the film. Promises of "temporary vegetable dye" didn't seem to mollify him.

Best Dog in a Television Series: Brigitte

Starring in: *Modern Family* (TV series)

In between scenes, Brigitte didn't hide out in some trailer. She got in plenty of puppy playtime with her best pal and understudy, Beatrice. Good thing she kept

---

...water lilies. But only those that grew in a pond by his house.

in shape. The French Bull dog had to learn to swim for Season 3. Not bad for a dog with no previous acting experience or even an obedience school diploma.

Best Dog in a Reality Series: (two winners)
Winner 1: Giggy
Starring in: *The Real Housewives of Beverly Hills*
Besides his tuxedo collar, Giggy arrived at the awards ceremony in a purple velvet body suit. Perhaps he should have skipped the collar. When his owner/co-star Lisa Vanderpump put him down for his moment in the spotlight, the pocket-sized Pomeranian toppled over.

Winner 2: Hercules
Starring in: *Pit Boss*
To convince the director that a pit bull would not go into attack-to-kill mode on the set, Hercules had to audition with a kid actor. When Hercules lay down and nuzzled the kid nose-to-nose, the dog won over everyone, even the director

Best Dog in a Direct-to-DVD Film: Rody
Starring in: *Marley and Me: The Puppy Years*
In Hollywood, connections help. Take Rody, the golden Lab puppy that starred as Marley, "the world's worst dog," in his puppy phase. Rody's owner, Michael Damian, happened to direct the film. Still, Rody showed true talent for ripping, chewing, and devouring everything in sight. (He probably rehearsed at home.)

FINDING FIRE

Most Native American tribes have legends about how they acquired fire. Here's one from the Cherokee nation about a smart and courageous little creature.

Long ago there was no fire on Earth. The animals spent a lot of time shivering in the cold. They could see fire in the sky. They knew that it could warm them. But the selfish Thunders were keeping it all to themselves.

One day, lightning hit a sycamore tree. The tree caught fire. The animals saw the smoke and the flames, and they got very excited. But they still had a problem: the fire was on an island in the middle of a lake.

"Who should we send to bring back the fire?" asked the council. Every animal that could fly or swim wanted to be the first to go.

White-feathered Raven stepped forward. "I am very strong," said Raven. "I will go."

"Very well," the council members agreed.

Raven soared to the island with ease. He swooped down to the burning tree, ready to grasp a flaming branch in his strong claws or beak. But the closer Raven flew, the hotter the fire raged. He could not get close enough to snatch a fiery branch. In fact, all he managed to do was scorch his beautiful white feathers, turning them as black as charcoal. (And they have been that way ever since.)

There's been a hurricane raging continuously on Jupiter for more than 300 years.

Buzzard went next. He got close enough to grab a burning coal, but it was too hot to carry in his beak or talons. He placed the coal on his head and began to fly back. As he flew, the fiery coal burned off his feathers. Buzzard dove to the lake and stuck his sizzling head into the water. (To this day, Buzzard has no feathers atop his head.)

The owls tried next, but a blast of fiery air stopped their flight. Screech Owl came back with eyes that had turned red from the heat. Hoot Owl and Horned Owl had white rings around their eyes from the ashes. (Yes, they look like that to this day.)

Next, a little green snake swam across the water to the island. He snatched a burning branch and placed it on his back. The branch burnt his skin. (And Green Snake has been Black Snake ever since.)

The animals did not know what to do. The fire was burning low. Soon it would be out.

"I will get the fire," said Water Spider.

The other animals laughed. "You can run across the water easily enough," they said. "But how will you carry the fire?"

"Like this," said Water Spider. She spun a thread from her body and wove it into a bowl. Then she fastened the bowl onto her back. While the other animals watched, she skittered across the lake. She took a tiny coal and placed it in the bowl. The bowl protected the coal from the water, and it protected Water Spider from the coal. Water Spider ran back across the lake and brought fire to the animals.

And that is how fire came to the animals and why Water Spider still carries her bowl on her back.

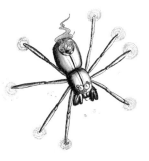

*   *   *

WHO KNEW?

Quite a few famous folks have, or claim to have, Cherokee ancestors, including these.

• Singer and actress Cher is part Cherokee through her mother, Georgia Holt.

• Legendary rock guitarist Jimi Hendrix was part Cherokee through his paternal grandmother, Nora Rose Moore.

• Steven Tyler, Aerosmith's lead singer, is part Cherokee through his mother.

• Actor Johnny Depp says, "I have Cherokee blood running through my veins." It somes from his great-grandmother, Minnie.

• Rosa Parks, the famous civil rights activist who refused to give up her seat on a bus, had mixed ancestry that included African-American, Scots-Irish, and Cherokee-Creek.

• He can't prove it, but former American President Bill Clinton claims that he is one-sixteenth Cherokee.

25 states get their names from Native American words.

CHIC TRASH

Most fashion designers think clothes should be made out of cotton, polyester, silk, or wool. But that doesn't mean everyone has such limited ideas.

DUCK YOUR DATE

Every year, the Duck brand duct tape company holds a "Stuck at Prom" contest. High school students around the country compete to make the most creative prom outfits possible using nothing but—you guessed it—duct tape. Entrants are judged on workmanship, originality, use of color, and accessories. Some students spend hundreds of hours *not* sewing their outfits. They make fake flowers, pieces of jewelry, and even shoes out of duct tape. Turns out, duct tape clothes are easy to make. "After you make an outfit out of duct tape, you'll never want to sew again!" said one entrant.

A SWEET PROJECT

In 2008, high school senior Molly Burt-Westvig got the idea to make a dress out of candy wrappers—specifically, Skittles wrappers. Why? Because she loves rainbows. Molly spent weeks eating Skittles. She fed them to her friends, and asked people to send her their empty wrappers. "I don't even like Skittles," she said. "Only the red ones." Molly pulled an all-nighter to make her dress. It took 15 hours and 101 wrappers.

Twice as many text messages are sent by girls as by boys.

YOU'VE GOT MAIL

If you pull hard enough on a soda-can tab, it comes clean off. That pop-top design is courtesy of Ernie Fraze, who invented both pull-top cans and fold-back tabs. Back in the '70s, soda drinkers littered the ground with discarded tabs, but one man had a different idea. In 1970, New Yorker Gonzalo Chavez felt inspired by chainmail armor. He started filing down pop-top edges and linking the tabs together with silver thread. Chavez spent hours in his workshop. He made pop-top vests, belts, skirts, and dresses, to wear and to sell. "They fit like a second skin," he said.

TRASHY DUDS

Paper or plastic? Some crafty people have figured out a new way to recycle a stash of plastic grocery bags—wear them! Plastic on its own is icky, grippy, and not breathable. But when you turn it into fabric, that all changes. To do that, stack six to eight layers on top of one another. Iron the layers between sheets of newspaper. Heat from the iron will fuse the plastic into a slick fabric. In 2006, art student Emily Berezin thought it might be fun to sew plastic-bag fabric into a dress and wear it grocery shopping. Result: "People gave me strange looks."

*　　*　　*

Priss: Whenever I'm in the dumps, I buy new clothes.
Sis: So—that's where you get them!

BIGFOOT'S COUSINS

Cryptids—legendary animals like Bigfoot and the Loch Ness Monster—have been sighted all over the world. See how many you can identify.

1. Ahool

a) A gigantic bat from the island of Java.

b) A snakelike sea monster seen near Alaska's Aleutian Islands.

c) A 30-foot-long lizard from the island of Madagascar.

2. Bessie

a) A huge vicious man-eating hog that lives in the wilds of Arkansas.

b) A very rare blonde female Bigfoot from Idaho.

c) A snake-like monster that lives in Lake Erie.

3. Zeuglodon

a) A giant man-eating Amazon-rainforest eagle.

b) A supposedly extinct snake-like whale that may be the true identity of many lake monsters.

c) A primitive species of man said to hide in the African jungles of Zaire, Zambia, and Zimbabwe.

4. Chupacabra

a) A hairy bloodsucking doglike creature with a taste for farm animals.

b) A Neanderthal-like hominid of western Siberia.

c) The flying monkey of Argentina.

5. Lusca

a) A many-armed sea beast resembling a giant octopus.

b) The elusive serpent of Switzerland's Lake Lucerne.

c) A leprechaun-like creature from Iceland.

6. Morag

a) A big-headed blood-sucking porcupine from Turkey.

b) A bog rat big as a bloodhound that hunts small lost children on the English moors.

c) Nessie's closest cousin, living in Loch Morar, 140 miles from Loch Ness.

7. Kongamato

a) The Apache name for Bigfoot.

b) A flying animal, perhaps a pterosaur, that lives in central Africa.

c) A giant mutated Japanese lizard said to attack Tokyo every 100 to 150 years.

8. Ucu

a) A 100-foot python from Uganda.

b) The South American Bigfoot.

c) A hawk with a 12-foot wingspan that preys on stray dogs and cats in China.

Answers on page 286.

PEACHY WEATHER

More odd things that fall from the sky.

• On October 25, 1947, fish fell from the sky in Marksville, Louisiana. The morning was foggy and calm, but twisters had been in the area the previous day. The fish were dead but fresh, so some people collected them, cooked them up, and ate them.

• Huge amounts of straw fell on Dartford, England, in August 1963. "There was far too much of it for it to have been dropped from an airplane," said a police officer. The straw fell for more than an hour.

• There are trillions of stars in the sky, but star*fish*? Maybe. On April 21, 1985, starfish fell on St. Cloud, Minnesota. Testing showed that the starfish were natives of Florida—that's more than 1,700 miles away. Scientists think student pranksters may have tossed the starfish from a university tower. The 78 mph winds blowing at the time flew them across town—a distance of about a mile.

• On July 12, 1961, peaches fell in Shreveport, Louisiana. The fruits weren't ripe—they were hard and green and the size of golf balls. Workers at a construction site said they saw the peaches falling from a thick cloud overhead.

• In 1982, corn kernels began to fall in Evans, Colorado. And they continued to fall occasionally for several years. One resident claimed that he'd been shooting them into the air with a slingshot. No one believed him.

• Residents of Dublin, Ireland, took cover from falling hazelnuts on May 9, 1867. A reporter wrote that "so violent was the force with which they descended that even the police, protected by unusually-strong head covering, were obliged to seek shelter."

• In June of 1911, Arlene Moyer got caught in a sudden storm while walking along the banks of Oregon's Sandy River. Instead of getting wet, she found herself being pelted on the head with salamanders. They were "falling from the sky, literally covering the ground and wriggling and crawling all over," she said.

How to tell if a cranberry is ripe: it will bounce.

IT'S ALIVE!

The past: Weird creatures were created in mad scientist's labs in sci-fi books and movies. The present: Weird creatures are being created in real science labs around the world.

SUPERSOLDIER ANTS

In 2006, supersoldier ants with huge heads and giant jaws invaded Long Island, New York. They were up to three times as big as other ants of the same species. Were they escapees from a film set? Nope. Scientists believe they may be throwbacks to ant ancestors that lived millions of years ago. "Birds with teeth, snakes with fingers, and humans with apelike hair—these are ancestral traits that pop up regularly in nature," explains Dr. Ehab Abouheif, a researcher in Evolutionary Developmental Biology at McGill University.

Dr. Abouheif says supersoldier ants are rare in nature. They've mostly been found in the southwestern United States and Mexico. So how'd they end up in Long Island? Dr. Abouheif decided to see if he could create his own supersoldiers in the lab. It was pretty easy. He covered ant larvae with juvenile growth hormones. Result: giant supersoldier ants.

GLOWING KITTENS

Scientists at the Mayo Clinic have created a new ally in the fight against feline AIDS—green glowing kittens. They injected monkey genes proven to block HIV into cat eggs. Kittens born from those eggs (and their offspring) were immune to feline AIDS. How can you spot an immunized kitten? Inject jellyfish genes into the cat eggs, too. That causes the cat's cells to glow an eerie green. Since the virus that causes feline AIDS is similar to the virus responsible for human AIDS, experiments with green glowing kittens means good news for battling this deadly disease.

SINGING MICE

In 1925, J.L. Clark discovered a mouse in his Detroit home. It sounded a lot like a bird that he had donated to scientists at the University of Michigan. University scientists tried to use Clark's mouse to breed a species of singing mice. They were unsuccessful, and the experiment was ended. In 2010, scientists at Japan's University of Osaka unveiled a lab-created singing mouse. The mouse was a result of their "Evolved Mouse Project." Scientists involved in the study bred mice that were prone to mutations to see what might evolve. They carefully checked each newborn mouse for anything odd. "One day we found a mouse that was singing like a bird," says lead researcher Arikuni Uchimura. They bred the singing mouse, and now they now have more than 100 singing mice.

"I know it's a long shot, and people would say it's 'too absurd'…but I'm doing this with hopes of making a Mickey Mouse some day," said lead researcher Arikuni Uchimura.

PLAYING RETRO

Grandma Uncle John used to say, "If you're bored, go outside and find something to do." Here's what she had in mind.

GRANNY GOTTA ROCK

Modern dolls look like real human babies. They can talk, burp, move, drink, and some can even pee. But if you want to really play retro, pick up a rock. "Our dolls were just big long rocks," says one elderly grandma. "We'd get a long rock and we'd say, 'Oh, I'm just so tired of carrying my baby,' just like we'd heard women say." Believe it or not, rocks are good for a lot more than just lugging around like babies. Even Granny would think these rock games rock:

GAME: *Kongki noli* (similar to jacks)
PLAYED BY: Kids in Korea
TO PLAY:

1. Find five small stones or pebbles.

2. Throw all of them down on the floor.

3. Pick one up with your fingers and toss it into the air. As you catch the one you tossed, pick up another rock. Continue, picking up each rock in turns.

4. On the second round, pick up two stones at a time.

5. On the third round, pick up three of them, then pick up the last one. On the fourth and final round, pick up four rocks.

Wait! You're not done yet! For the last step, toss the stones into the air and catch them on the back of your hand. Snatch them off and try to catch them in your palm. The number you catch is your score.

GAME: *Stealing Rocks*
PLAYED BY: Kids in Texas
TO PLAY:

1. Divide into two groups and take places on opposite sides of a line drawn across a field.

2. Place piles of small rocks, equal in number, several yards from the center line.

3. Every kid on each side has to break across the line and touch a rock without being tagged by the enemy.

4. If the player is tagged before reaching the pile, he must stand on the enemy's base until a player from his own side tags him out.

5. If the player makes it to the enemy's pile before he's tagged, he can take a rock back to his team's pile.

6. The game ends when one side has all the rocks.

GRANNY GOTTA STICK

Even more versatile than rocks, sticks can be used as musical instruments, swords, kite-building materials, or outdoor drawing tools (when dirt is the paper). With a few other supplies, you can turn sticks into fishing poles, flags, forts, sculptures, and rustic dolls. "A favorite baby doll of ours was nothing but a stick of wood wrapped up in an old coat or something," says one old-timer.

GAME: *Hoop and Stick*
PLAYED BY: African-American kids who grew up on slave plantations
TO PLAY:

Stand a hoop up, and then roll it along the ground with the stick—no hands allowed. (You could try the same game with a stick and a Hula Hoop.) For more fun, challenge a friend to a stick-and-hoop race.

GAME: *Dandi Biyo*
PLAYED BY: Kids in Nepal
TO PLAY:

1. Find one stick that's about two feet long and another stick that's about six inches long and pointed at one end.

2. Dig a hole about four inches deep in the ground, and lay the small stick across it.

3. Then put one end of the big stick in the hole and do your best to jerk it in a way that will fling the small stick into the air.

4. If the other player can catch the small stick before it hits the ground, your turn is over—if not, you get to keep going.

*　　*　　*

THAT'S A FACT!
Rats can hold their breath for three minutes and tread water for three days.

THE MAN WHO BATHED IN A HAT

Tired of the same old bathroom routine? Try these!

TAKE A HARD HAT-BATH

While fighting forest fires, Ole Wik learned to take a bath using just a few cups of water—in his firefighter's hard hat. "It's possible to clean every part of your body but your hair," said Wik. Wik's hard-hat bath secret: Don't use soap.

PEE IN THE SHOWER

A Brazilian environmental group wants to get people to conserve water. How? By peeing in the shower. Urine is 95% water anyway, so peeing in the shower is harmless. If you pee in the shower just once a day—instead of flushing the toilet—you can save 1,157 gallons of water each year. The group even made a cartoon video to promote the idea. It shows cartoon people and characters—a kid, a basketball player, a frog, the Statue of Liberty, and a space alien—all urinating in the shower. The video ends with kids' voices saying, "Pee in the shower! Save the Atlantic rainforest!"

Sony's first ever product: an electronic rice cooker.

MOAT OF DEATH

In case you'd like to grow your own island, here's how.

KILLER GODDESS

In the South Pacific Ocean, 20 miles east of a string of islands known as American Samoa, lies an active undersea volcano called Vailulu'u. The summit of Vailulu'u contains an oval-shaped caldera more than a mile wide and 1,300 feet deep. In 1999, the floor of the caldera was nearly flat. But by 2005, something amazing had happened. A 1,000-foot-tall volcanic cone had risen inside the crater. Scientists named the cone *Nafanua* for the Samoan goddess of war.

FEAST FOR WORMS

Between the crater walls and the cone, scientists discovered a deadly secret: a "moat of death." Vents within the smoldering volcano had pumped hot water laced with chemicals into the moat. Day after day, the toxin levels rose. The result: an acidic, deep-sea danger zone.

With water as hot as 180°F, the toxic circle kills almost every living thing that comes close. The rotting bodies of fish, squid, and crustaceans litter the deadly circle. Only one lifeform has defied the odds to survive and thrive: bright red, acid-resistant bristle worms called *polychaetes*. They glide through the poison and feast on the bacteria of decomposing sea creatures.

CHAIN, CHAIN, CHAIN

Nafanua now lies 2,300 feet below sea level, but the cone is slowly growing towards the ocean's surface. Growth comes from the release of "pillow lava." Hot magma squeezes out of cracks in the ocean floor, like toothpaste from a pressurized tube. When the magma hits the cooler water, it hardens or congeals into large blobs of new rock known as "pillows."

"If you keep squirting toothpaste from one place, the squirts will overlie one another," said Hubert Staudigel from the Scripps Institution of Oceanography in California. The release of pillow lava adds height and width to the cone. With enough pillows, Nafanua might eventually become a new island and the Samoan Island chain could add a new link. Scientists say it could happen in just a few decades.

*   *   *

HELLO, SPACE!

In 2012, California seventh-grader Laruen Rojas used a do-it-yourself balloon kit to launch her Hello Kitty doll into space. Hello Kitty soared skyward in a silver rocket, but the balloon did all the work. She reached an altitude of 93,625 feet, high enough for the onboard camera to send home beautiful pictures of Earth. Then pressure from the upper atmosphere caused the balloon to burst (as planned) and Hello Kitty parachuted home. Her ship landed in a tree where it dangled and pinged until recovered by an Earthling who was recorded saying, "Oh, dude!"

ANIMAL ANTICS

Never underestimate an animal's resourcefulness.

E XTRA CHEESE, PLEASE
Authorities in British Columbia, Canada, have
been trying to track down a thief with a big
appetite for pizza. The perp was first spotted going
through the trash outside Fat Tony's pizza parlor in
Whistler Village around dinnertime on a Monday.
Later, the same villain came inside and grabbed a beef-
and-blue cheese pizza right off the counter. Employees
watched in horror as he ate the whole pizza (plus three
more) and left...without paying a cent. No one tried to
stop him. Why not? The pizza-loving perp was a bear.
Conservation officers are considering setting a trap for
the bear outside the restaurant. (Maybe they should try
an extralarge pepperoni with extra cheese.)

WHY FLY?

Transport officials in Stockholm, Sweden, are keeping
watch on a group of passengers taking free rides on the
city's subway. Rasmus Sandsten, a spokesman for the
Mass Transit Railway, said they get on at Farsta Strand
and ride to the Farsta Centrum Shopping Center, one
stop away. There's a reason the MTR is paying such
close attention: The freeloading riders are a flock of
pigeons. They stand calmly at the platform and wait
for the train to arrive, then hop aboard. It seems to

be a one-way trip. "We haven't been told of as many incidents of pigeons on the tube on the way back, so we think they fly back," Sandsten said.

MUTT MUNCHIES

Some dogs will eat just about anything—grass, bones, smelly socks, and, according to some kids, homework. Christy Lawrenson's Labrador-chow-bulldog mix, Tuity, ate something her owner didn't want to lose: an envelope filled with ten $100 bills. Lawrenson had left the envelope on the counter to take to the bank later that day. When her husband came home for lunch, the envelope was gone and shredded $100 bills littered the house. A guilty Tuity sat nearby. Mr. Lawrenson induced the dog to vomit the cash, and was able to recover nine of the $100 bills—which the bank replaced. The tenth bill had too many serial numbers missing to make it valid. The couple sent the mutt-chewed money off to the Department of the Treasury with an explanation— *sorry, the dog ate it*—hoping to get that last bill replaced.

...and his last (*A View to a Kill*) at age 58.

NAME THAT DINOSAUR!

Have you ever wondered why dinosaur names are so hard to pronounce? Here's the answer!

WHAT'S YOUR SPECIES?

It all started with Carl Linnaeus, an 18th century Swedish scientist with an international vision. Linnaeus thought every animal should have a universal name. One that scientists could use, no matter which language they spoke. He created a system that named all the animals in Latin. All living things were given two basic Latinized names that showed their relationship to all other living things. Each group of animals had a genus name. And each individual in the genus had a species name.

In his book *Dinosaurs: The Most Complete, Up-to-Date Encyclopedia for Dinosaur Lovers*, paleontologist Thomas Holtz used crocodiles as an example. "When we say crocodile in English, we're actually talking about a genus called *Crocodylus* in the Linnaean system," he writes. After the genus name, each *Crocodylus* species has a unique second name. For example, *Crocodylus niloticus* is the common Nile crocodile. And *Crocodylus porosus* is the saltwater crocodile.

Obdormition is the scientific term for when a limb "falls asleep."

FIT FOR A KING

The Linnaean system caught on. Over time, some dino-namers took the naming game seriously. Others picked up a bit of knowledge about Latin endings, and then came up with really goofy names. Here are just a few.

• Barnum Brown, a famous turn-of-the-century paleontologist, discovered *Tyrannosaurus rex* in 1902. It was the biggest *Tyrannosaurus* unearthed, so the name "rex"—the Latin word for "king"—was a perfect fit.

• Flying reptile *Arthurdactylus conan-doylensis* was named in 1994 for famous mystery author Sir Arthur Conan Doyle. Conan Doyle is best known for his Sherlock Holmes stories. But this name was a tribute to his 1912 novel, *The Lost World*, which featured a forgotten South American land where dinosaurs survived extinction.

• When a new species of sea creature called a trilobite was found in 1995, it was called *Aegrotocatellus jaggeri*, after Mick Jagger, the lead singer of the legendary rock band the Rolling Stones. (Our sources say *Aegrotocatellus* means "sick puppy" in Latin.)

CLASSIC GAMER TRIVIA

Do you eat, sleep, and breathe video games? Then this glimpse into video gaming history is for you.

MARIO BROS.

Mario got his start in video games in 1981. Nintendo video game creator Shigeru Miyamoto gave him a walk-on in his *Donkey Kong* arcade game.

- Ever wonder why Mario wears a hat? Because hair was really hard to create using 1980s graphics tech.

- Mario was originally a carpenter called Jumpman. But Nintendo's U.S. office wanted a better name for the American release of the game. While staff members were trying to think up a new name, they were interrupted by their landlord...*Mario* Segale.

- In 1982's *Donkey Kong, Jr.*, Mario was a bad guy. He even had a twirled moustache to highlight his evil nature.

- Before he was transformed into a terrorizing turtle, evil-doer Bowser was an ox.

- Chain Chomp bad guys in *Mario Bros. 3* were inspired by a mean dog that chased Miyamoto as a kid.

Traditional Maori greeting in New Zealand: rubbing noses together.

LEGEND OF ZELDA

- *The Legend of Zelda* was first released in 1986, but only in Japan for the Nintendo Famicom disk system. The original title? *The Hyrule Fantasy: Legend of Zelda.*

- Link, the hero of the Legend of Zelda games, is left-handed.

- In the Forest of Temples, players meet four sisters—Jo, Beth, Amy and Meg. They are named after the main characters in Louisa May Alcott's novel, *Little Women.*

- Actor and comedian Robin Williams named his daughter Zelda after the video game.

POKÉMON

- *Pokémon* was released by Nintendo in 1996 for their hand-held Game Boy system.

- In Japan, *Pokémon* is called *Pocket Monsters.*

- *Pokémon* has a yearly national championship in the United States. After the 2012 event, top players and their Pokémon teams became part of the Pokémon World Tournament feature in *Pokémon Black Version 2* and *Pokémon White Version 2.* The feature allows players to compete against the actual 2012 champs.

- The most valuable Pokémon trading card is a rare holofoil Pikachu "Illustrator" card. Only six of them were made—for a magazine contest prize—and they are worth up to $20,000 each.

GIRLS IN SPORTS PART II

On pages 70–71, we shared more than two thousand years of girls playing to win. Here's how female jocks kept moving forward (or backward) in the world of sports.

• **1896.** A woman named Melpomene is banned from running in the first modern Olympics in Athens, Greece. Why? Officials said, "It is indecent that the spectators should be exposed to the risk of seeing the body of a woman being smashed before their very eyes."

• **1904.** Bertha Kapernick becomes the first woman to give rodeo bronco-busting a try at the Cheyenne, Wyoming, Frontier Days celebration.

• **1907.** Underwater ballerina Annette Kellerman shocks New York City by wearing a one-piece bathing suit. A year later, she is arrested for "indecency" in the Boston Harbor for a suit that exposed her bare legs.

• **1931.** Baseball Commissioner Landis bans women from professional baseball after 17-year-old pitcher Virne Beatrice "Jackie" Mitchell strikes out both Babe Ruth and Lou Gehrig in an exhibition game. The ban holds until 1992.

• **1950.** Twelve-year-old Kathryn Johnson plays for the King's Dairy Little League Baseball team in Corning,

New York. She cuts off her braids and calls herself Tubby to try out for the team. Girls are later banned.

• **1960.** Wilma Rudolph—nicknamed the "Black Gazelle" for her graceful running style—becomes the first American woman to win 3 track-and-field gold medals in a single Olympics.

• **1970.** Pat Palinkas holds the ball for the Orlando Panthers' kicker, becoming the first woman to "play" in a professional football game.

• **1972.** President Nixon signs Title IX legislation into law, making it illegal to exclude girls from school sports based on their gender.

• **1977.** Lusia Harris becomes the first female drafted by a NBA team (the New Orleans Jazz)...without the pick being voided by the league.

• **1998.** Christina Sanchez is the first female matador welcomed into Madrid, Spain's *Les Ventas* bull-fighting ring.

• **2012.** Near the end of the game, high school backup quarterback, Erin DiMeglio, becomes the first girl in Florida history to play quarterback in a varsity high school football game.

DAREDEVIL OF NIAGARA FALLS

Fearless or crazy? The world's greatest tightrope walker took his life into his hands (and feet) on a weekly basis.

GORGING ON FAME

Monsieur Blondin—the world-famous acrobat—was attempting his most hair-raising performance ever. The tightrope walker was crossing the Niagara Gorge on a three-inch rope. He'd done it before, but this time was different: He was carrying another man on his back! "Below the two men the thunder of the falls roiled up and the ghostly mist wreaths curled up and swam around them," wrote a reporter. "Each step seemed a step nearer to death."

The rope stretched 1,100 feet from the American side of the gorge to the Canadian side. Nearly 200 feet below, the roaring waters of the Niagara River rushed by at 42 miles an hour. Thousands of people had gathered to watch the crossing. The tightrope rippled in the wind. It sagged about 20 feet in the center.

"The rope swayed gently from side to side as Blondin walked and it gave slightly at each step forward." Falling from the rope would mean certain death for Blondin and the man he was carrying.

NO FEAR?

Blondin was the stage name of Jean-François Gravelet, a French entertainer who got his new name from his blond hair. He'd been a talented acrobat as a kid, displaying agility, grace, and balance like none other. A famous French gymnast named Ravel encouraged him to travel the world, showing off his skills. Eventually, Blondin joined a troupe of acrobats and came to the U.S.

"I was a rope-walker at four," Blondin said. "I have never felt fear—no, not even when crossing Niagara."

On a visit to Niagara Falls, Blondin got the idea to walk across the gorge. He left the acrobatic troupe and went into business for himself. He hired a manager named Harry Colcord, and planned for his first crossing.

DAREDEVIL TRICKS

On June 30, 1859, thousands of people gathered to watch that first attempt. Clad in silk tights, Blondin stepped onto the tightrope, carrying a 26-foot pole to help him keep his balance. Watchers may have expected the young man to scurry across the rope as quickly as possible. Not so. Instead, he stopped along the way to lie down for a moment. Then he stood and did a backward somersault before continuing on his way. After reaching the Canadian side, Blondin walked back along the rope with a camera, taking pictures. And if that wasn't enough, he carried out a chair, balanced it on the rope, and stood on it.

WEEKLY SENSATION

News spread quickly. Blondin began making weekly crossings on the rope, drawing large crowds. His stunts included crossing while walking backward, riding a bicycle, pushing a wheelbarrow, walking on stilts, and wearing a blindfold. He even crossed in the dark.

Blondin challenged himself to take on ever-harder stunts. But carrying a man on his back was the biggest risk of all. Though he tried to persuade several men to accompany him, no one would agree. Just one look into the gorge was enough to scare them off.

Finally, Blondin asked his manager to make the crossing. "Harry," he said, "you're a small man like myself. I can carry you. Be a good fellow and come along." Before Harry Colcord could make up his mind, Blondin announced to the press that it would happen.

ROPED IN

Colcord was terrified as he climbed onto Blondin's back. At 5 feet 5 inches tall and 140 pounds, Blondin wasn't a big man. Colcord weighed slightly less: 136 pounds. That meant Blondin would be carrying his own weight…on his back…while walking on a tightrope swaying above a raging falls.

Around 100,000 spectators watched as Blondin stepped onto the rope. "The vast multitude was motionless with awe and foreboding," wrote a reporter for *The New York Times*. "The cliffs and surrounding points of observation were black with people."

The tips of Blondin's balancing pole were whipping up and down in the treacherous wind. Then some of the guy ropes snapped from the strain. The report in *The New York Times* said, "Men's faces whitened as they breathlessly watched the two men swaying on the rope. Many men and women fainted."

NOT YET!

As they reached the point where the guy ropes extended from the Canadian side, Colcord began to feel a sense of relief. But the worst was yet to come.

"Finally Blondin's foot was planted on the knot that joined the lines," Colcord said. "I was sucking in some air when suddenly the rope was jerked from beneath Blondin's feet." Somehow, Blondin regained his balance. Dripping with sweat, he raced to the finish.

The crossing took half an hour, but finally they reached the safety of the Canadian side. One man who helped them down from the rope exclaimed, "I wouldn't look at anything like that again for a million dollars!"

*   *   *

PLANET PIXAR!

Fast facts about Pixar, the animation studio that brought you Monsters, Inc.; Up; *and the* Toy Story *movies.*

• The Pizza Planet truck that Woody and Buzz use to hitch a ride in *Toy Story* appears in every Pixar film except *The Incredibles*.

• The Pixar development team came up with ideas for *Monsters, Inc.*; *Finding Nemo*; *A Bug's Life*; and *WALL-E* at a single lunch meeting.

• Pixar employees are encouraged to play and relax at work. Seriously? Yep. They play video games, swim, get massages, play volleyball or basketball, compete in air hockey or Ping-Pong games, and use scooters to get from place to place…all during the work day.

• Because *WALL·E* relies so much on visual storytelling (instead of speech), the movie's crew picked up some tips from old-time silent film stars. For a year and a half, they spent their lunchtimes watching every single Buster Keaton or Charlie Chaplin movie ever made.

• Pixar was originally the computer graphics division of Lucasfilm. Steve Jobs bought the division in 1986 and named it Pixar. Jobs asked employee John Lasseter to create animated commercials to promote computer hardware. Lasseter's animation proved to be far more popular than Jobs' hardware. Pixar landed a deal with Disney to produce computer-animated films. And the rest is animation history!

• For *Brave*, Pixar's animators crafted 350 custom brushes in Photoshop—all just for adding detail to moss and rocks! Some of the computerized brushes have rough, granite-like patterns on them. Others are smoother and wavier. Layering in details using different brushes allowed animators to create very realistic scenery.

• The *Toy Story* film crew wanted mean kid Sid from the original movie to reappear in *Toy Story 3*. But they knew his bitter temperament would not have served him very well in life. So, while Andy goes off to college, Sid is shown working as a garbage man.

• The *Up* animation team produced only about four seconds of animation per week while making the film. Total production time? Five years.

• On the final day of work for the 58-person animation crew of *Toy Story 3*, director Lee Unkrich led a mini-marching band through the Pixar studio. In the band: two snare drummers, two bass drummers, two giant monkeys, and a Yeti.

EYE-OPENING EGYPTIANS

*Believe it or not, the makeup used in ancient Egypt might
have been healthier than what you can buy today.*

I LOVE MAKEUP

When you think of ancient Egyptian queens like
Cleopatra or Nefertiti, you probably picture thick
black swoops of eyeliner going nearly to their temples.
It gave their eyes a distinctive almond shape. But it may
have had a purpose beyond beauty.

The basis of the eyeliner was a
mineral called lead sulfide, also
known as *galena*. Lead-based
substances can be toxic, but a
recent scientific study showed
that galena can boost the
immune system. Scientists now
believe that Egyptian eyeliner
could have prevented infections
and also helped treat them.

The Egyptian makeup kit of
5,000 years ago also contained:

• Ground henna leaves, to color nails
and lips reddish-orange. Henna is still
used today to make hair dyes, and is

considered safer than modern petroleum-based dyes.

• Moisturizers made from animal fat, olive oil, and crushed leaves and flowers. These creams softened the skin and protected it from the harsh sun and wind.

• Rouge made from ochre, a reddish clay, to give the cheeks a "blush."

• Flowers, plants, and seeds, crushed and made into perfumes with animal fat and plant oils. One perfume, called Cyphi, contained 16 ingredients, including honey, wine, raisins, sorrel, myrrh, cardamom, and juniper. Cyphi was said to help a person sleep and to ease stress and strain.

SCRAMBLED OSTRICH EGGS, ANYONE?

Since she was Queen of the Nile (Denial, get it?), Cleopatra might have plastered this ancient Egyptian anti-wrinkle cream on her face…if she'd lived more than 39 years.

Directions: Mix the ingredients—if you can find them. Apply the cream to your face, and then leave it on for six days.

• Whipped ostrich eggs

• Bullock's bile (digestive acid from a young bull)

• Refined natron (salt)

• Milk

• Incense

• Olive oil

• Crushed cyperus (an herb)

• Wax

MAMMOTH BURGERS

Some people will eat anything! Here's the proof.

A REAL MOUTHFUL

Mammoths have been extinct for about 4,000 years. Most of the great woolly beasts died at the end of the last Ice Age, about 10,000 years ago. But sometimes a frozen one is found—preserved in ice for thousands of years. Every once in a while, someone decides to turn a frozen mammoth into a meal. Here's the problem: A dead animal begins to decay almost immediately. To be truly preserved—and safe to eat— an animal would have to freeze very quickly.

Herbert Hoover, U.S. President during the Great Depression...

The average woolly mammoth stood 11 feet tall at the shoulder. An adult weighed from 6 to 8 tons. That's a big chunk of meat. "Even in the harshest conditions, it would take hours for the several-ton body of a mammoth to freeze solid," wrote science journalist Richard Stone in his book *Mammoth: The Resurrection of an Ice Age Giant.* "That would allow ample time for bacteria to begin to putrefy the meat." Eating putrid meat? Bad idea.

If a dying mammoth fell into a body of water, it might freeze quickly. If it fell on land, Stone says, its carcass would have to be covered by a heavy snowfall to freeze. If it wasn't, warm temperatures could spoil it. Winds and dry air would dehydrate it, turning the meat into mammoth jerky.

NOT-SO-PERMA FROST

Most frozen mammoths have been found in Siberia. During the last great Ice Age, huge herds of woolly mammoths roamed this Arctic region of Russia. "It's so cold that the frozen soil, called *permafrost,* has acted as a giant freezer," says mammoth researcher Christopher Sloan. Permafrost never thaws, not even in summer.

Until now. Thanks to global climate change, the Siberian permafrost is beginning to melt. Mammoth carcasses are coming out of their long deep freeze. Some scientists believe that thousands of them lie beneath the soil, just waiting to be found. Of course, most finds yield bones and tusks, not fast-frozen meat. Reports say that 50 tons of mammoth bone turn up every year in

Russia—and the number keeps growing.

FROZEN FOODS

In 1901, members of the Russian Academy of Sciences heard about an unearthed mammoth near the banks of Siberia's Berezovka River. They launched an expedition to see it. A few expedition members were curious to know what mammoth meat would taste like. In the end, they couldn't eat it. It was the smell: Apparently, after a few thousand years in the deep freeze, mammoth meat smells like a dirty stable mixed with rotten organs.

"The meat was dark red, suggesting horse meat, and marbled with fat," said one member of the expedition. "The dogs ate it avidly. The men could not quite steel themselves to try it."

Sometimes mammoth meat isn't eaten out of curiosity. It's eaten out of necessity. In 1872, *The New York Times* ran a story about French explorers who were trying to reach the North Pole. For a time they survived on nothing but mammoth meat they had uncovered. They ate it "broiled, roasted, and baked."

Sound yummy? Probably not. The USDA's food safety guidelines say "freezing keeps food safe almost indefinitely." But, 1) we don't think they were talking about thousands of years, and 2) meat that old will have freezer burn that looks like grayish-brown leather, and tastes like it, too.

*   *   *

MISSED TRANSLATIONS

Some translations into English are so bad they're funny!

• An Italian ad campaign for Schweppes Tonic Water translated the product's name as "Schweppes Toilet Water."

• When the Pope visited Miami, an American T-shirt company wanted to print shirts for its Spanish-speaking customers. Instead of saying "I Saw the Pope," the Spanish translation read, "I Saw the Potato."

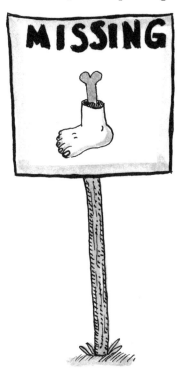

• In China on a woodsy hiking trail with steep drop-offs, a sign cautions tourists to "Beware of missing foot."

• A sign outside of a zoo in Budapest, Hungary, read: "Please do not feed the animals. If you have any suitable food, give it to the guard on duty."

YOU CALL THAT ART?

These artists might be stretching the definition of "art" a bit too far. You decide.

ARTIST: Rachel Betty Case
MEDIUM: Toenail clippings
THE ART: This Easton, Pennsylvania, artist makes tiny sculptures of animal skeletons and insects—entirely of what she calls "human ivory." (Most of us call it "nail clippings.")

"It amazes me that this is a part of our body that people trim and discard," Case said. "To me, nails are more beautiful than that."

The sculptor's work is sold at the Mütter Museum in Philadelphia and on Coney Island. If you have the cash and will ship nail clippings to her, she'll create a custom sculpture using your very own nail clippings.

ARTIST: Cosimo Cavallaro
MEDIUM: Cheese
THE ART: In 2001, armed with a rented sprayer and five tons of expired pepper-jack cheese, this New York artist created the "Cheese House." He found an abandoned house in Powell, Wyoming, that was due to be torn down. The local Chamber of Commerce gave

---

Smells funny: *dysosmia* is the scientific name for foul-smelling.

him the okay to turn it into art. Cavallaro sprayed on the cheese, coating the house inside and out. The feat took him about a week to complete.

The house wasn't Cavallaro's first step into cheese-covered art. He started in 1999 with his father's armchair. His dad took one look at it and asked, "Why?" But his mother laughed. "People who get it laugh," said Cavallaro.

Since then, Cavallaro has coated a jacket, a pair of shoes, a New York hotel room, and even the iconic 60's fashion model Twiggy with ooey-gooey cheese. But he doesn't want to be known as "the cheese guy." He's also worked in ketchup, chocolate, and ham.

ARTIST: Zhu Cheng
MEDIUM: Giant Panda poop
THE ART: With the help of a dozen 11-year-old students, sculptor Zhu Cheng created a reproduction of the famous armless Greek statue known as the *Venus de Milo*. Zhu collected Giant Panda poop from the Chengdu Research Base of Giant Panda Breeding. He mixed the poop with vegetable glue to create "clay." Zhu's team of students filled a 24-inch clay mold of the naked goddess with the panda-poo clay. Zhu says the sculpture was meant to show the "internal conflict between beauty and waste." Chinese culture places a high value on the Giant Panda. But Giant Pandas produce a lot of waste—about 45 pounds of poo per day. In 2010, Zhu's sculpture sold to a retired Swiss diplomat for the price of 300,000 yuan—$45,113.

JURASSIC FARTS

*What can long-necked dinosaurs teach us
about global warming? It's a gas!*

WHO FARTED?
In 2012, two British scientists, Dave Wilkinson and Graeme Ruxton, revealed a startling discovery about dinosaur times. They were trying to figure out why the climate was so warm and wet when dinosaurs roamed Earth. Their conclusion: sauropod farts.

Fartosaurus

The scientists announced their dino-fart theory in the respected science journal *Current Biology*. They chose their words carefully: "Our calculations suggest that sauropod dinosaurs could potentially have played a significant role in influencing climate through their methane emissions." (At the BRI, we know that's a polite way to say, "Sauropods changed the climate by farting.")

GASSY GIANTS

Sauropods were the biggest land animals to ever live on Earth. They had huge bodies, long necks, and puny heads. They first appeared in the late Triassic period (about 230 million years ago), had a heyday in the Jurassic period (200 to 145 million years ago), and went extinct at the end of the Cretaceous period (about 65 million years ago). Among the many sauropods were *Apatosaurus*, *Brachiosaurus*, and *Argentinosaurus*, which weighed up to 100 tons. (African elephants, the largest land animals alive today, average about 4 to 6 tons.)

Sauropods were herbivores (plant eaters). Scientists think they probably ate ferns, gingkoes, conifers, and similar plants. To maintain their size, they had to eat fast (they gulped their food without chewing it). And they had to eat a lot. How much? An 11-ton elephant can eat about 1,000 pounds of plant matter a day. Scientists say a 77-ton dinosaur would have had to eat at least four times that much, or 4,000 pounds of plants every day.

FART MATH

Scientists believe a sauropod's digestive system was a lot like a cow's. Because they don't chew, cows have four special stomachs to help digest their food. The long digestive process produces methane gas, and some of that gas comes out as burps and farts. Wilkinson and Ruxton did the math: given their size, giant sauropods could have produced more than 500 million tons of methane gas per year. "Our calculations suggest that these dinosaurs could have produced more methane than all modern sources—both natural and man-made—put together," said Wilkinson.

Fingernails grow four times faster than toenails.

BATMAN RULES!

BAM, BOFF, SOCK, CRASH, POW, ZAP, SPLATT!
Now that we have your attention...

Those are the words most people remember from the 1960s Batman TV series. But sometimes Batman (Bruce Wayne) stopped biffing long enough to utter lines meant to educate his young sidekick Robin (Dick Grayson). Hint: It helps to imagine a serious square-jawed man wearing a unitard, a bat mask, and a cape saying these lines.

Batman: Better put five cents in the meter.

Robin: No policeman's going to give the Batmobile a ticket.

Batman: This money goes to building better roads. We all must do our part.

Robin: You can't get away from Batman that easy!

Batman: Easily.

Robin: Easily.

Batman: Good grammar is essential, Robin.

Dick: Gosh, economics is a dull subject.

Bruce: Oh, you must be jesting, Dick. Economics dull? The glamour, the romance of commerce. It's the very lifeblood of our society.

Dick: What's the use of learning French anyway?

Bruce: Language is the key to world peace. If we all spoke each other's language, perhaps the scourge of war would be ended forever.

Dick: Gosh, Bruce, yes. I'll get these darn verbs if they kill me!

Bruce: Most Americans don't realize what we owe to the ancient Incas. Very few appreciate they gave us the white potato and many varieties of Indian corn.

Dick: Now whenever I eat mashed potatoes, I, for one, will think of the Incas.

Batman: Robin, you haven't fastened your safety bat-belt.

Robin: We're only going a couple of blocks.

Batman: It won't be long until you are old enough to get a driver's license, Robin, and you'll be able to drive the Batmobile and other vehicles.

Remember motorist safety.

Robin: Gosh, Batman, when you put it that way.

Robin: We'd better hurry, Batman.

Batman: Not too fast, Robin. In good bat-climbing, as in good driving, one must never sacrifice safety for speed.

Robin: Right again, Batman!

Robin: Picked up the seal pulsator yet, Batman?

Batman: We're still over land, Robin, and a seal is an aquatic, marine mammal.

Robin: Gosh, yes, Batman! I forgot.

Robin: That's an impossible shot, Batman.

Batman: That's a negative attitude, Robin.

CELEBRITY KIDS' NAMES

We remember celebrities' names because they're famous.
But you'll remember the names of these celebrity kids
because they're just plain weird.

• Pop star Ashlee Simpson and Fall Out Boy bassist Pete Wentz welcomed their first child into the world with the name Bronx Mowgli Wentz. (Yes…his initials are BMW.)

• Comedian/magician Penn Jillette and his wife, Emily, named their daughter Moxie Crimefighter. Jillette said that they chose the name so that when she's pulled over for speeding, she can tell the officer that they're on the same side. Moxie's younger brother is named Zolten, which also happens to be the name of Dracula's dog.

• Actor Rob Morrow and Debbon Ayer named their daughter Tu. As in Tu Morrow…get it?

• Actress Shannyn Sossamon named her baby boy Audio Science. (Maybe she had him confused with a stereo brand found at Radio Shack.)

• When actor Jason Lee and wife Beth Riesgraf had a baby boy, they named him Pilot Inspektor. They got the name Pilot from a song by indie rock band Grandaddy, which includes the lyrics "He's simple, he's dumb, he's the pilot."

• We're not sure what made singer/songwriter Frank Zappa give his children the names Moon Unit, Dweezil, Diva Thin Muffin Pigeen, and Ahmet Emuukha Rodan. But we hope they find a way to pay him back.

• Actor David Duchovny and his wife, Téa Leoni, named their son Kyd. Guess yelling, "Hey, Kyd!" keeps things simple.

• Michael Jackson named his first two children Prince Michael and Paris Michael Katherine. By the time his second son was born, he must have been out of ideas. He named the baby Prince Michael II. But he did give the baby an original nickname—Blanket.

• Not to be outdone in the realm of royal names, Michael Jackson's brother Jermaine named his own son Jermajesty.

• Former heavyweight boxer George Foreman named each of his five sons George: George Jr., George III, George IV, George V, and George VI. He thought about naming his five girls George as well, but decided not to. Instead, he named them Michi, Freeda George, Georgetta, Natalie, and Leola. (Guess he couldn't resist squeezing a few more Georges in there.)

*   *   *

"Like Superman, I too have a Fortress of Solitude. Only mine flushes."

—**Jerry Thomas**

ANSWERS

Outhouse Logic (from page 64)

The easiest way to solve this logic puzzle is to make a chart that includes all of the possibilities, like this:

	RED	YELLOW	BLUE	GREEN
BRADY	X	X	O	X
MARCIA	O	X	X	X
LUKE	X	O	X	X
JADE	X	X	X	O

Start by putting an O in the spaces we know. Jade is the youngest, since Marcia is the oldest and the boys are both older than Jade. So she uses the green one. Since a sister uses the red one, that must be Marcia. Put an O in that space. Put an X in any space that can't work. Brady never goes after dark, he can't use the red one, which is used at midnight. Luke and Jade can't be red, since Marcia claimed that one. And Brady, Marcia, and Luke can't be green. We can also X out all the other possibilities for Marcia and Jade. All that's left are Brady and Luke. Since there's no music in the blue outhouse, harmonica-playing Luke must take the yellow one. That leaves Brady in the blue outhouse.

The Poop Quiz (from page 88)

1. c); 2. b); 3. c); 4. a); 5. b); 6. c); 7. b); 8. c.

Gross Body Quiz (from page 127)

1. a) 1 pint; 2. b) 2 cups; 3. c) a softball; 4. c) 2 gallons;

5. a) 3; 6. a) 36 million.

Bacon Derby (from page 163)

To find the solution, go through the clues and start making a list. We know that Pinky finished behind Tulip: (TULIP, PINKY). We also know that Rosie beat Jade, but we can't tell if either of them beat Pinky or Tulip yet, so let's just hold onto that information. We learn that Tulip wore purple, which means that she finished behind the pig that wore yellow:

1. _____ = YELLOW; 2. TULIP = PURPLE

3. PINKY = _____

Jade did not win the race because she finished behind Rosie. Since Pinky did not finish last, she would have to be third, because she also finished behind Tulip. That makes Jade last, and Rosie first.

1. ROSIE=YELLOW; 2. TULIP=PURPLE

3. PINKY = _____; 4. JADE = _____

The pig in blue finished ahead of the pig in green. So that tells you the final colors: PINKY = BLUE, JADE = GREEN.

Phrase Origins (from page 172)

1. a); 2. c); 3. b); 4. a); 5. b); 6. a.

$1 Words (from page 199)

Each letter of the alphabet is "worth" its corresponding number—"a" is 1 cent, "b" is 2 cents, "z" is 26 cents, etc. And the $1 words? 1. grumpy, 2. turkey, 3. toilets.

Whose Nose? (Answers from page 203)

1. c; 2. e; 3. d; 4. f; 5. a; 6. b; 7. h; 8. g; 9. j; 10. i.

Bigfoot's Cousins (from page 244)

1. a) The ahool gets its name from the cry it supposedly makes while it flies in search of prey: *Ahooooool!* It's a fish eater with giant claws and a head like a monkey.

2. c) She's also known as South Bay Bessie and is said to be up to 40 feet long. Biologists think sightings have mostly been of lake sturgeon, a fish that can grow up to eight feet in length.

3. b) Also known as *Basilosaurus*, these whales were 55 to 75 feet long and are thought to have been extinct for more than 30 million years. Ogopogo—the famous lake monster of Canada's British Columbia—might be a zeuglodon.

4. a) Chupacabras are said to be about four feet tall with sharp fangs, no lips, and red eyes. They suck the blood out of chickens, goats, and other small farm animals in Mexico, Puerto Rico, and nearby countries.

5. a) Luscas are legendary residents of deep "blue holes" off the coast of the Bahamas. Some scuba divers claim to have been attacked by them and say the creatures also have shark-like qualities.

6. c) Descriptions of Morag sound a lot like Nessie.

7. b) Kongamatos are said to live in swamps and look like flying dragons. Some people believe they are pterodactyls.

8. b) Ucu is said to live at high elevations in the Andes Mountains.